MW00958931

# Google Tag Manager Certification

## A Comprehensive Guide to Google Tag Manager Certification

## Cybellium

Copyright © 2024 by Cybellium™. All rights reserved.

No part of this guide may be reproduced, distributed, or transmitted in any form or by any means, including photocopying, recording, or other electronic or mechanical methods, without the prior written permission of the publisher, except in the case of brief quotations embodied in critical reviews and certain other noncommercial uses permitted by copyright law.

For permissions requests, contact the publisher by email using this email address: admin@cybellium.com

This book is intended for informational purposes only. While every effort has been made to ensure the accuracy of the information provided, neither the author nor the publisher can be held responsible for any errors, omissions, or changes that may occur after publication.

The inclusion of businesses, services and other entities in this book does not imply endorsement or recommendation

# Table Of Contents

# 1. Introduction to Google Tag Manager Certification

The digital landscape is evolving at an unprecedented pace, and businesses are increasingly leveraging data to drive decision-making and improve their online presence. One of the pivotal tools in this data-driven ecosystem is Google Tag Manager (GTM). For digital marketers, web developers, and data analysts, mastering GTM is not just advantageous—it's essential. Achieving certification in Google Tag Manager demonstrates a comprehensive understanding of this powerful tool and its capabilities, setting professionals apart in an increasingly competitive market.

This chapter sets the stage for your journey towards Google Tag Manager certification. It will explore the significance of GTM in the current digital marketing landscape, elucidate the benefits of becoming certified, and provide an overview of what you can expect as you prepare for the certification process. From understanding the foundational principles of GTM to recognizing its strategic advantages, we aim to equip you with the necessary insights and knowledge to navigate the complexities of this tool with confidence.

Whether you're looking to enhance your technical skills, streamline your workflow, or provide added value to your organization, this introduction serves as your entry point into the world of Google Tag Manager. Let's embark on this educational journey together to unlock the full potential of GTM and position yourself at the forefront of digital marketing expertise.

# 1.1 Definition and Scope of Google Tag Manager

Google Tag Manager (GTM) is a tag management system (TMS) that allows users to easily add and manage marketing and analytics tags on their website or mobile app without having to modify and deploy the code directly. Introduced by Google in October 2012, GTM has since become an essential tool for digital marketers, data analysts, and web developers looking to streamline their tag management processes.

At its core, Google Tag Manager provides a user-friendly interface that abstracts away the complexities associated with coding and directly implementing tags. Tags are snippets of JavaScript or HTML that send information to third parties for purposes such as web analytics, advertising, and user experience improvements. For example, tags can be used to track visitor behavior, measure campaign effectiveness, or even monitor the performance of a particular webpage.

The scope of Google Tag Manager extends far beyond just adding tags. GTM offers a rich set of features designed to simplify and enhance the entire tagging process. One of the key features of GTM is its "container." A container is essentially a collection of tags, triggers, and variables that define when and how tags should be deployed. Once a container is created, it can be easily updated and republished, allowing for quick and flexible management of tags.

Triggers and variables are integral components within a GTM container. Triggers specify the conditions under which a tag should be fired. For instance, a trigger might be set to fire a tag when a user clicks a specific button or when a page view event is recorded. Variables, on the other hand, are used to store and retrieve dynamic information that can be employed by tags and triggers. Common examples of variables include URL parameters, Form IDs, or user-defined constants.

One of the significant advantages of using Google Tag Manager is its ability to improve website performance. By consolidating all tags into a single container, GTM reduces the need for multiple tag requests, which can often slow down a website. Moreover, since tags are managed through GTM's asynchronous loading, they do not block the rendering of the web page. This leads to faster load times and an improved user experience.

GTM also offers built-in debugging and preview modes, making it easier to test and verify tags before they go live. The preview mode allows users to see how tags will behave on a website without actually deploying them, thereby minimizing the risk of errors. Additionally, GTM comes with a comprehensive set of built-in tags for popular services such as Google Analytics, Google Ads, and others, streamlining the process even further.

Security is another critical aspect covered by Google Tag Manager. By providing a structured and centralized framework for managing tags, GTM minimizs the chances of security vulnerabilities that could arise from manually embedding third-party scripts. It also supports features like user permissions and version control, ensuring that only authorized users can make changes and allowing for easy rollback to previous versions if necessary.

Furthermore, GTM is designed to be highly scalable, accommodating the needs of both small businesses and large enterprises. Whether a website has a few dozen visitors or millions, GTM can efficiently handle the tagging requirements, making it a versatile solution for various organizations.

In summary, Google Tag Manager is a robust and versatile tag management system that simplifies the process of adding, editing, and managing tags on websites and mobile apps. It provides a user-friendly interface, enhances website performance, improves security, and offers invaluable features like debugging and preview modes. With its extensive scope and capabilities, GTM serves as an indispensable tool for marketers, developers, and analysts seeking to optimize their digital properties.

## 1.2 The Role of Tag Management in Digital Marketing Success

In an ever-evolving digital landscape, businesses continually seek ways to enhance their marketing strategies and execution. One often overlooked but crucial component that plays a significant role in digital marketing success is tag management. Tags are snippets of code, typically JavaScript, that are incorporated into web pages and function to facilitate the collection and transfer of data to various third-party services. These can include analytics platforms like Google Analytics, advertising networks such as Google Ads, CRM systems, and social media channels. Proper tag management leads to more efficient data collection, improved website performance, and more agile marketing initiatives.

At the most fundamental level, tag management is essential because it provides a systematic approach to implementing and handling tags. Without an organized tag management system (TMS), marketers and developers would need to manually insert and update the individual code snippets on multiple pages of a website, a task that is time-consuming, error-prone, and inefficient. A TMS, like Google Tag Manager, Adobe Launch, or Tealium, makes it easier to manage and update the tags from a single interface, thus substantially reducing human error and saving significant time.

One of the primary roles of tag management in digital marketing is improving data accuracy and consistency. Modern digital marketing relies heavily on data-driven decision-making. Data inaccuracies can lead to misguided strategies, resulting in wasted marketing budgets and missed opportunities. A TMS ensures that the deployed tags collect accurate, timely, and consistent data across all digital touchpoints by setting standardized rules and configurations. This level of reliability in data collection enables marketers to make more informed decisions and optimize campaigns effectively.

Another critical advantage of tag management lies in the considerable improvement of website performance. Often, improperly managed tags can lead to slow website loading times. When tags are arbitrarily or cumulatively added to a website without coordination, they can conflict with one another or cause an unnecessary drain on server resources. Tag Management Systems offer features like tag sequencing, which ensures that tags load asynchronously without delaying the rendering of the critical content on the page. This improved efficiency can lead to faster website performance, which is a significant factor for search engine optimization (SEO) and user experience.

Moreover, tag management offers a significant boost to marketing agility. The digital marketing environment is dynamic, often requiring rapid changes to campaigns and data collection methods. In the absence of a TMS, implementing new tags or modifying existing ones necessitates input and intervention from the IT department, leading to delays and bottlenecks. With TMS, marketers can autonomously manage the tags, making real-time adjustments to campaigns without the constant need for technical support. This agility ensures that marketing initiatives are always up-to-date and aligned with current strategies and market conditions.

Enhanced compliance and security are other pivotal roles of tag management. With increased scrutiny on data privacy regulations like GDPR in Europe and CCPA in California, non-compliance can lead to severe penalties and reputational damage. Tag Management Systems provide robust governance features such as user permissions, tag versioning, and centralized control, ensuring that all tags comply with prevailing data regulations. These features offer an added layer of security by reducing the risk of unauthorized modifications and ensuring that only vetted and approved tags are deployed on the website.

Finally, TMS plays a role in amplifying the effectiveness of A/B testing and personalization initiatives. Robust digital marketing strategies often rely on experimentation and personalized content delivery to enhance user engagement and conversion rates. By efficiently managing and controlling the tags associated with various tracking and personalization tools, a TMS enables seamless monitoring of user interactions and behaviors. The insights gained through such methods help tailor marketing messages and website content, contributing to a more personalized and effective user experience.

In conclusion, the role of tag management in digital marketing success cannot be overstated. From ensuring data accuracy and improving website performance to enhancing marketing agility and compliance, tag management forms the backbone of effective and efficient digital marketing strategies. As businesses strive to maintain a competitive edge in a crowded digital marketplace, leveraging a robust TMS will undoubtedly remain a cornerstone of their success.

## 1.3 Historical Perspectives on Tag Management

The evolution of tag management systems (TMS) reflects broader changes within the digital marketing and analytics landscapes, intertwining with advancements in web technologies and shifts in user behavior. Understanding the historical perspectives on tag management illuminates the motivations behind its inception, development, and the pivotal milestones that shaped its current form.

In the early days of the internet, digital marketers primarily relied on static HTML pages and a limited range of website tracking tools to analyze user behavior. Tags—snippets of code inserted into web pages—were one of the earliest methods for collecting data on website usage, user interactions, and campaign performance. These early tags were often hard-coded directly into the website's HTML by developers, making the process cumbersome and rigid. Even minor changes required developer intervention, leading to project bottlenecks and inefficiencies.

As websites grew more complex and dynamic, the need for a more streamlined method to implement and manage tags became evident. Around the late 1990s and early 2000s, the advent of tag management systems marked an industry shift—these systems were designed to centralize and simplify tag deployment. By providing a container tag that could encompass multiple individual tags, TMS platforms allowed marketers to add, edit, and remove tags without extensive coding or developer assistance.

The early TMS platforms were rudimentary compared to today's sophisticated solutions, but they addressed significant pain points. Digital marketers could now implement tags more swiftly, decreasing time-to-market for campaigns and granting greater agility. The reduction in dependency on IT departments also meant that marketing teams had more control over their tracking mechanisms and data collection strategies.

During the mid-2000s, the growing importance of data privacy and the rise of regulations, such as the European Union's General Data Protection Regulation (GDPR), necessitated further evolution in tag management. Compliance requirements pushed TMS providers to incorporate features that allowed for better control over data collection practices, consent management, and user privacy. This period saw the development of more advanced user interfaces and enhanced functionalities, including audit trails and version control, which provided transparency and accountability.

By the late 2000s, the explosion of digital marketing channels, including social media, mobile apps, and video platforms, further accelerated the complexity of

Cybellium - Google Tag Manager Certification

tag management. Tags were no longer solely about website data—they encompassed pixel tracking for social media advertising, event tracking for mobile applications, and various other third-party integrations. TMS platforms evolved to become more comprehensive, supporting a wide range of tag types and providing advanced functionalities like conditional triggers and data layer integration.

Data layers, introduced in the early 2010s, represented a significant leap in tag management technology. A data layer serves as a structured storage of key information about the site and users, simplifying the process of passing relevant data to different tags. By using data layers, marketers could ensure consistent and accurate data was being sent to their analytics and marketing tools, thus enhancing data quality and reliability.

The emergence of cloud-based TMS solutions also marked a pivotal moment. Cloud technology offered scalability, performance improvements, and easier updates. Leading companies like Google with Google Tag Manager, Adobe with Adobe Launch, and Tealium with Tealium iQ spearheaded the move towards robust, cloud-based tag management systems, offering more intuitive user interfaces, extensive native integrations with other digital marketing tools, and enhanced capabilities around data governance and security.

The historical trajectory of tag management thus mirrors the broader digital transformation narratives: from static, developer-centric processes to agile, marketer-driven solutions with sophisticated governance and compliance features. As we look forward, the future of TMS will likely be influenced by ongoing developments in technology, regulatory changes, and ever-evolving user expectations, continuing to adapt and grow to meet the needs of digital marketers in a rapidly changing landscape.

# 1.4 Key Concepts in Tag Management

Tag management is an essential aspect of digital marketing and web development, as it enables the efficient deployment and control of various JavaScript-based tags on a website. Tags are snippets of code added to web pages to integrate third-party tools for tasks like analytics, marketing, and advertising. By centralizing the management of these tags, businesses can ensure better website performance, enhance data accuracy, and streamline workflows.

One of the primary key concepts in tag management is the Tag Management System (TMS). A TMS is a software solution that simplifies the process of implementing, handling, and maintaining tags on websites without needing in-depth coding knowledge. This not only empowers marketing teams to quickly deploy and update tags but also reduces dependency on developers, thereby accelerating the implementation process and fostering a more agile marketing environment.

Centralization of tag management is another critical concept. Before the advent of TMS, developers had to manually embed tags directly into the website's HTML code. This fragmented approach often led to version control issues, redundant tags, and increased page load times. With a TMS, all tags are managed from a single interface, offering a holistic view of all deployed tags. This centralization helps in maintaining consistency, improves governance, and ensures that tags are correctly implemented throughout the website.

Data Layer is a fundamental component in the effective use of a TMS. The data layer is a structured JavaScript object that holds information about the web page and the user interactions within it. It acts as an intermediary between the website and the tags, providing a consistent and reliable source of data for all tags. By using a data layer, businesses can decouple the website's functionality from the tagging structure, making it easier to manage complex data requirements without altering the website's core code.

Rules and Triggers form the backbone of tag deployment within a TMS. Rules define the conditions under which tags should be fired. These conditions could be based on various factors such as user behavior, page URLs, or specific events like button clicks. Triggers, on the other hand, are specific events or actions that need to occur for a tag to be activated. The combination of rules and triggers ensures that tags are only deployed when necessary, thereby optimizing their performance and relevance.

Another important concept is Version Control. A TMS typically offers versioning capabilities, allowing users to create and manage different versions of their tag configurations. This feature is crucial for testing and validating changes before deploying them to the live website. In case an issue arises, reverting to a previous version can be done seamlessly, minimizing the risk of disruptions and ensuring continuous website functionality.

Tag Auditing and Debugging are essential practices in maintaining the integrity of a tag management system. Tag auditing involves regularly reviewing the tags to ensure they are up-to-date, correctly implemented, and not causing conflicts. Debugging tools within a TMS allow users to test tags in a controlled environment, identifying and rectifying issues before they affect the live site. Effective auditing and debugging practices help maintain data quality and contribute to the overall performance of the website.

Consent Management is increasingly becoming a significant part of tag management due to growing concerns about privacy and data protection. With regulations like GDPR and CCPA, businesses need to ensure that user consent is obtained before deploying certain tags, especially those related to tracking and analytics. A TMS can integrate with consent management platforms to control the firing of tags based on user consent preferences, thus ensuring compliance with legal requirements.

Lastly, Collaboration and User Permissions within a TMS facilitate teamwork and ensure that the right individuals have appropriate access levels. Administrators can assign roles and permissions to different users, ensuring that only authorized personnel can make changes to tag configurations. This not only enhances security but also promotes accountability within the team.

In conclusion, effective tag management is about leveraging a TMS to centralize, streamline, and optimize the deployment of tags on a website. Understanding these key concepts is crucial in managing tags efficiently, ensuring data accuracy, compliance with legal standards, and ultimately, enhancing the overall performance and functionality of a digital marketing strategy.

# 2. The Google Tag Manager Ecosystem

In the ever-evolving digital landscape, the ability to effectively manage and deploy various marketing and analytics tags is paramount for organizations striving to maintain a competitive edge. This is where Google Tag Manager (GTM) steps in, offering a robust platform that simplifies the otherwise intricate process of tag management. As a cornerstone of modern digital marketing strategies, GTM empowers businesses to seamlessly integrate and manage a multitude of tags without the need for extensive coding knowledge, thereby streamlining workflows and enhancing overall efficiency.

In this chapter, we will delve into the multifaceted ecosystem that constitutes Google Tag Manager. We will explore its core components, from tags, triggers, and variables to containers and workspaces, and illustrate how they intertwine to facilitate a cohesive tag management system. By comprehending the structural nuances and operational dynamics of GTM, you will gain invaluable insights into leveraging this powerful tool to its fullest potential, thereby optimizing your digital marketing efforts and driving substantive business outcomes. As we embark on this journey, clarity and precision will serve as our guiding principles, ensuring that each concept is meticulously articulated and easily comprehensible.

## 2.1 Components of Effective Tag Management

Effective tag management is a crucial aspect of modern digital marketing and data analytics. It involves the strategic deployment, organization, and automation of tags on digital properties such as websites and mobile applications. Tags are snippets of code added to a website or app to collect specific data, monitor user behavior, and engage in various marketing activities. When managed properly, tags can provide essential insights into user interactions, optimize marketing campaigns, and ensure compliance with privacy regulations. The components of effective tag management include a well-structured tag management system (TMS), proper tag governance, efficient data layer implementation, regular audits and monitoring, collaboration between teams, and adherence to data privacy standards.

A robust tag management system (TMS) is the foundation of effective tag management. A TMS is a platform that allows marketers and developers to easily manage and deploy tags without extensive coding knowledge. Popular TMS platforms include Google Tag Manager, Adobe Experience Platform Launch, and Tealium. Utilizing a TMS simplifies the process of adding, updating, and removing tags, reducing the reliance on IT departments and minimizing the risk of errors. A TMS also provides a centralized interface for managing all tags, ensuring that they are organized and consistent across all digital properties.

Proper tag governance is essential for maintaining an organized and efficient tag management strategy. Governance involves defining clear policies and procedures for tag implementation, approval, and maintenance. This includes establishing naming conventions for tags to ensure they are easily identifiable and categorizing tags based on their purpose (e.g., analytics, marketing, and functionality). It also involves setting up user roles and permissions to control who can create, modify, or delete tags. Effective governance helps prevent tag sprawl, reduces the risk of data discrepancies, and ensures that tags are used appropriately to drive business goals.

Efficient data layer implementation is another critical component. A data layer is a JavaScript object that stores and standardizes the information collected by tags before it is sent to various marketing and analytics tools. By using a well-structured data layer, organizations can ensure that data is consistently and accurately captured across different tags and platforms. This improves data quality and enables more sophisticated tracking and analysis. A well-implemented data layer supports better decision-making and enhances the overall performance of digital marketing efforts.

Regular audits and monitoring of tags are vital to maintaining the integrity and effectiveness of tag management. Audits involve reviewing the tags currently deployed on digital properties to ensure they are functioning correctly and collecting accurate data. This process helps identify and fix any issues, such as broken tags, duplicate tags, or unauthorized tags. Monitoring tools can track tag performance and load times, alerting teams to any anomalies that could affect the user experience or data accuracy. Regular audits and monitoring ensure that the tag management strategy remains aligned with business objectives and compliance requirements.

Collaboration between different teams—such as marketing, IT, and data analytics—is essential for effective tag management. Each team brings unique expertise and perspectives to the table, ensuring that tags are deployed in a way that meets technical requirements, business goals, and user experience standards. Effective communication and collaboration help streamline the tag implementation process, resolve issues quickly, and foster a culture of continuous improvement. Cross-functional collaboration also ensures that all stakeholders are aware of and can contribute to the organization's data strategy.

Lastly, adherence to data privacy standards is a non-negotiable component of effective tag management. With regulations like GDPR, CCPA, and others, organizations must ensure that their tag management practices comply with legal requirements. This includes obtaining user consent before collecting data, providing transparent information about data collection practices, and ensuring that data is securely stored and processed. A TMS can help manage consent mechanisms and automate compliance-related tasks, reducing the risk of violations and building trust with users.

In conclusion, effective tag management is a multifaceted process that requires a combination of technology, governance, and collaboration. By implementing a robust TMS, establishing clear governance policies, utilizing a well-structured data layer, conducting regular audits, fostering collaboration, and adhering to data privacy standards, organizations can optimize their digital marketing efforts and achieve better data quality and compliance.

## 2.2 The Role of Tags, Triggers, and Variables

The intricate world of digital analytics and marketing hinges on the precise collection, management, and utilization of data. Fundamental to this ecosystem are three pivotal components: tags, triggers, and variables. Each serves a distinct yet interdependent role in ensuring that data is comprehensively gathered and accurately interpreted. Understanding the functions and interplay of these elements is crucial for optimizing digital marketing strategies, refining user experiences, and making data-driven decisions.

Tags are essentially snippets of code embedded within a website or mobile application to collect and share data with third-party platforms such as Google Analytics, Facebook Pixel, or advertising networks. These tags can track a wide array of user interactions, ranging from page views and clicks to form submissions and video plays. They serve as the foundation for data collection, enabling marketers to gather insights on user behavior, campaign effectiveness, and website performance. Tags are the starting point in the data collection process, triggering the capture and transmission of data points to specified destinations for analysis.

Unlike tags, which primarily focus on data collection, triggers act as the activation mechanism for these tags. Triggers define the conditions under which a tag should be fired. For instance, a marketer may set a trigger to fire a specific tag when a user reaches a thank you page after a successful purchase or clicks on a particular call-to-action button. Triggers can be set to a wide range of conditions, including page URL, button text, form completion, or custom events defined by JavaScript. The nuanced control offered by triggers ensures that tags are deployed only when relevant actions occur, thereby enhancing the precision of data collection.

Variables add another layer of complexity and functionality to this process. They act as placeholders or containers that store dynamic values to be used by tags and triggers. Variables can capture and pass values like user IDs, transaction amounts, or product categories. For example, a variable might pull the value of a user's membership status from a cookie to determine if they should receive certain promotional tags. The flexibility of variables allows marketers to create more sophisticated and personalized tagging structures. By dynamically pulling in values at runtime, variables make it possible to create contextually relevant tags and triggers, thereby tailoring data collection to specific user journeys and business metrics.

The interplay among these three elements can be likened to a well-choreographed dance. When a user interacts with a website, variables capture relevant data points, which are then evaluated against the pre-defined conditions of triggers. If these conditions are met, the corresponding tags are fired to collect and transmit the data. This fluid interaction ensures that only pertinent information is captured and analyzed, facilitating more accurate insights.

Moreover, the integration of tags, triggers, and variables within tag management systems like Google Tag Manager has streamlined the process significantly. Tag management systems provide a centralized platform where marketers can deploy, manage, and test tags without requiring extensive coding knowledge or direct modifications to the website's backend. This not only accelerates deployment times but also reduces the risk of human error, enhances website performance, and ensures compliance with data privacy regulations.

To sum up, the roles of tags, triggers, and variables are indispensable in the realm of digital analytics and marketing. Tags act as the data collectors, triggers determine the conditions under which data is gathered, and variables provide the dynamic values necessary for contextual accuracy. Their cohesive interaction forms the backbone of a robust data strategy, enabling organizations to derive meaningful insights, optimize user experiences, and drive informed decision-making. The integration of these elements within tag management systems further amplifies their efficacy, underscoring their importance in the evolving landscape of digital marketing and analytics.

## 2.3 The Influence of Data Layer on Tag Management

The concept of tag management has become crucial in the realm of digital marketing, analytics, and website optimization. As businesses increasingly depend on data-driven decisions, the need for effective tag management becomes essential. A pivotal component that greatly influences tag management practices is the data layer. The data layer serves as a bridge, facilitating seamless communication between a website's operational elements and various tag management systems (TMS). In this context, understanding the influence of the data layer on tag management is instrumental for optimizing data collection, governance, and actionable insights.

Firstly, the data layer acts as a central repository where all necessary data points are systematically placed. This uniformity simplifies the process for tag management systems to extract and utilize data. Without a well-structured data layer, data points could be scattered across different parts of a website, making extraction cumbersome and error-prone. This centralized approach ensures that all tags, whether for analytics, marketing, or other purposes, can pull consistent and accurate data from a single location. Consequently, it reduces the redundancy and complexity associated with data collection, enhancing the efficiency of tag management.

Secondly, the data layer enhances the flexibility and scalability of tag management. As businesses grow and evolve, so do their data needs and the intricacies of their web ecosystems. A robust data layer structure allows for easy modifications and expansions without overhauling the existing tag management setup. For example, if a company decides to integrate a new marketing tool or analytics service, the data required by this new service can be readily appended to the data layer. The TMS can then be configured to pick up the new points from the data layer, making the process seamless. This adaptability ensures that businesses can swiftly respond to technological advancements and market demands without being bogged down by complex rewiring of their tag management infrastructure.

Furthermore, the data layer profoundly influences the accuracy and precision of data captured by various tags. By defining clear structures and standardized naming conventions within the data layer, businesses can mitigate risks associated with inconsistent data collection. For instance, customer interaction data, transaction details, and user behavior metrics can all be defined with precise variables in the data layer. This precision ensures that the data tags capture is clean and standardized, reducing discrepancies and enhancing the reliability of analytics and reporting tools. Accurate data is the cornerstone of informed decision-making, and a well-architected data layer is crucial in maintaining this accuracy.

Moreover, the data layer plays a significant role in simplifying the governance and compliance aspects of data management. In an era where data privacy regulations like GDPR, CCPA, and others are becoming stringent, having a clear and organized data layer enables businesses to manage consent and data usage effectively. The data layer can include user consent status and preferences, which tags can then reference to ensure compliance with regulatory requirements. This centralized approach not only simplifies the execution of data governance policies but also fortifies a business's position in adhering to global data protection standards.

Another important aspect of the data layer's influence on tag management is in debugging and troubleshooting. When issues arise in data collection or tag firing, a well-structured data layer can make it significantly easier to diagnose and resolve these issues. The transparency provided by a standardized data layer allows developers and analysts to trace data flow and pinpoint the exact stage where a problem might have occurred. This streamlined troubleshooting saves time, reduces downtime, and ensures that marketing and analytics operations are not unduly interrupted.

In conclusion, the data layer is a vital foundation that profoundly enhances the efficacy and robustness of tag management. By centralizing data points, enhancing flexibility, ensuring accuracy, aiding in compliance, and simplifying debugging, the data layer serves as an indispensable element in the orchestration of effective tag management strategies. Businesses that harness the full potential of a well-structured data layer can expect to see improved data integrity, operational efficiency, and ultimately, more insightful and actionable business intelligence.

## 2.4 The Impact of Privacy and Data Protection on Tag Management

With the explosion of digital marketing and e-commerce, tag management systems (TMS) have emerged as a critical tool for organizations seeking to streamline the deployment and management of marketing tags. Tags are snippets of code embedded in websites that help to collect and share data with third-party services for purposes such as analytics, advertising, and personalization. While TMS simplifies the process of managing these tags, it also raises significant concerns around privacy and data protection.

The increasing use of TMS necessitates a stringent focus on privacy and data protection regulations, such as the General Data Protection Regulation (GDPR) in Europe and the California Consumer Privacy Act (CCPA) in the United States. These regulatory frameworks impose strict requirements on organizations regarding the collection, use, and sharing of personal data. Compliance with these regulations impacts how tags are managed, as they often collect personal identifiable information (PII) or data that could be deemed sensitive.

One of the most immediate impacts of privacy regulations on tag management is the requirement for explicit user consent before data can be collected. Under GDPR, organizations must obtain unambiguous consent from users before deploying any tags that track or collect personal data. This necessitates the implementation of consent management platforms (CMPs) that can work alongside TMS to ensure that tags are only activated once consent has been given. The integration of CMPs with TMS adds an additional layer of complexity, but it is essential for compliance and for maintaining user trust.

Data minimization principles, another cornerstone of privacy regulations, also significantly affect tag management. Organizations are required to collect only the data that is necessary for the intended purpose. This principle forces organizations to critically evaluate each tag and its functional necessity, thereby reducing the amount of data collected and limiting data exposure. This may involve the pruning of unnecessary or redundant tags, a practice that not only aligns with data protection principles but also enhances site performance and loading speeds.

Another critical aspect is data protection by design and by default, which mandates that privacy considerations be integrated into the design and operation of systems, including TMS. Tag configurations must be designed to adhere to privacy rules from the outset. This may involve anonymizing data collected by tags, ensuring secure transmission of this data, and restricting access to authorized individuals. Encryption and other data security measures should be in place to protect data both in transit and at rest.

Incidents of data breaches have highlighted the importance of robust data protection measures in tag management. Given that tags often relay data to multiple third-party services, each of these interactions represents a potential vulnerability. Organizations must ensure that all third-party services receiving data via tags employ sufficient safeguards to protect user data. This may involve conducting regular audits and risk assessments to verify the security measures implemented by third-party vendors.

Furthermore, the transparency obligations under privacy regulations necessitate that organizations provide clear, concise information about their data collection practices, including the use of tags. Privacy policies and notices should explicitly mention what data is collected via tags, the purposes for which it is used, and the third parties with whom the data is shared. This empowers users to make informed decisions about their data.

Lastly, the evolution of browser privacy features poses additional challenges and changes to the landscape of tag management. Browsers like Safari, Firefox, and Chrome have incorporated features that block or limit tracking capabilities of certain tags. These browser-level interventions are often more stringent than regulatory requirements and have prompted organizations to adapt their tag strategies. Server-side tagging is one of the emerging solutions in response, which shifts the tracking and data collection processes to servers, thereby reducing reliance on client-side tags that are susceptible to browser restrictions.

In summary, the impact of privacy and data protection on tag management is profound and multifaceted. Organizations must navigate a complex web of regulations and implement comprehensive measures to ensure compliance while leveraging the benefits of tag management systems. This entails obtaining explicit user consent, adhering to data minimization principles, integrating privacy into the design of tag management processes, ensuring data security, maintaining transparency, and adapting to evolving browser privacy features. The careful balancing of these elements is essential for safeguarding user privacy and maintaining the integrity and efficiency of digital marketing operations.

# 3. Understanding Tag Management Processes

In the digital age, the ability to effectively manage and deploy marketing and analytics tags is more crucial than ever for businesses aiming to optimize their online performance. This intricate process, known as tag management, involves the organization, implementation, and monitoring of tiny bits of code, often referred to as tags, that are embedded into a website or mobile application. These tags collect valuable data and facilitate a myriad of functions, from tracking user behavior to delivering personalized content and ensuring compliance with various privacy regulations.

Understanding the intricacies of tag management processes is not just for IT professionals or digital marketers; it's an essential skill for anyone involved in online business strategy. These processes streamline workflows, enhance data accuracy, and improve website load times, driving more efficient and effective marketing campaigns. However, the actual implementation can be complex, requiring a thorough grasp of both the technical and strategic dimensions.

In this chapter, we delve into the core elements of tag management, exploring the lifecycle from initial tag creation and deployment to ongoing maintenance and optimization. We will demystify the components that make up a robust tag management system, outline best practices, and examine various tools available in the market that can support your tag management efforts. As we navigate through this topic, you will gain a clear and comprehensive understanding of how to harness the power of tag management to advance your digital objectives.

# 3.1 The Tag Management Lifecycle: Creation, Deployment, and Testing

The process of managing digital tags on a website or app can be intricate and multidimensional, often paralleling the lifecycle management that one might associate with a traditional software development project. This can be categorized into three primary phases: creation, deployment, and testing. Each of these stages plays a critical role in ensuring the successful implementation and maintenance of tags, which are essential for tracking user interactions, gathering analytics data, and optimizing digital marketing campaigns.

In the initial phase, creation, the focus is on developing and configuring the tags to meet specific tracking and data collection needs. This involves understanding the requirements of various stakeholders, such as marketing teams, data analysts, and web developers. The specifications often come from predefined metrics and key performance indicators (KPIs) that the organization aims to measure.

During the creation stage, tag management solutions (TMS) like Google Tag Manager, Adobe Launch, or Tealium iQ are commonly used. These tools provide a user-friendly interface for creating tags without the need for extensive coding. Nonetheless, a deep understanding of JavaScript and the Document Object Model (DOM) remains beneficial, especially when creating custom tags or more complex tracking solutions. The creation phase will also include setting up data layers, which serve as a structured and consistent way to pass data from the website or app to the tags and, ultimately, to the analytics platform.

Once the tags are created and configured, the next stage is deployment. Deployment is the process of pushing the newly created tags to the live environment where they will begin collecting data. Prior to full deployment, tags are often tested in a staging environment to ensure they function as intended without causing disruptions to the website's primary activities. In the absence of thorough testing, tags can inadvertently slow down page load times or, worse, break critical functionalities of the website.

In deploying tags, the deployment method is of utmost importance. One common approach is asynchronous loading, which allows tags to load independently of other page elements. This prevents tags from hindering the loading speed of essential content. The use of container tags, a concept facilitated by most TMS tools, is another strategic approach, allowing multiple tags to be managed in a consolidated manner, reducing redundancy and enhancing control.

Switching to the testing phase, this is arguably the most critical part of the lifecycle. Testing ensures that tags are not only firing correctly but also tracking the data as intended. Various testing methods can be utilized, including manual checks, automated testing, and using built-in preview and debug tools provided by most TMS platforms. A sound testing plan should include a mix of these methods to cover different aspects of tag performance.

Manual testing often involves simulating user interactions to see if tags are triggered appropriately. Automated testing, on the other hand, can offer more thorough and repeatable checks for validity and functionality. Tools such as Selenium or custom scripts can be programmed to verify that tracking codes are firing under different conditions and user scenarios. Built-in preview and debug tools allow testers to view which tags would fire on a given page and check the data being sent to the analytics platform.

Moreover, ongoing monitoring is essential even after tags have been tested and deployed. Tag health monitors can help in detecting any issues in real-time by ensuring tags continue to fire as expected and do not gather inaccurate data. Maintaining vigilance through continuous testing cycles helps in catching any discrepancies early, allowing for timely corrections.

In conclusion, managing the lifecycle of tags involves meticulous planning, skilled execution, and rigorous testing. The creation of tags should be driven by clear business objectives and thorough documentation, allowing for ease of maintenance and updates. Deployment must ensure efficiency and minimal disruption, while comprehensive testing guarantees the reliability and accuracy of data collection. By adhering to these principles, organizations can effectively leverage tag management to support their broader digital analytics and marketing strategies.

## 3.2 The Role of Debugging in Effective Tag Management

Debugging is an indispensable component in the realm of tag management, serving as the linchpin that ensures efficacy, reliability, and accuracy in data tracking and reporting. In a landscape where enterprises increasingly depend on digital analytics to inform strategic decisions, the precision of data collection mechanisms cannot be overstated. Debugging serves to identify and rectify errors, optimize performance, and confirm the integrity of tags, making it a vital practice in effective tag management.

At its core, debugging in tag management involves scrutinizing the deployed tags to ensure they are functioning as intended. Tags are snippets of code embedded in web pages or mobile applications, capturing interactions and relaying this data to analytics platforms for analysis. Given their pivotal role in the data ecosystem, any malfunctions or inaccuracies in tags can cascade into flawed data, leading to misguided business decisions. Thus, the primary function of debugging is to catch these errors before they infiltrate the analytics reports.

The process typically starts with validation. Ensuring that each tag has been correctly implemented is the first step. Tools like browser developer consoles, tag debugging tools, and specialized tag management systems often provide real-time inspection capabilities. These tools allow for the examination of network calls, checking if tags are firing correctly and verifying the parameters being sent. URLs, event names, and custom dimensions or metrics should all be vetted to ascertain their accuracy.

Once validation is confirmed, the next phase involves diagnosing issues. Errors in tags can stem from a variety of sources - syntax errors in the code, misconfigured triggers, or conflicts with other scripts on the page. Debugging tools often highlight code inconsistencies and show detailed messages that point towards the origin of the problem, making it easier for developers to pinpoint and address the issue.

Beyond fixing evident errors, debugging also plays a pivotal role in performance optimization. Tags can add latency to page load times, affecting user experience and potentially lowering the page's search engine ranking. By analyzing the sequence and load times of tags, managers can rearrange or defer tag loading to optimize performance. For instance, non-critical tags can be set to load asynchronously or only after the main content has rendered, ensuring a smoother and faster user experience.

Debugging further ensures compliance with data privacy laws and regulations. Tags often handle sensitive user data, and mishandling this data can lead to severe legal repercussions. Debugging tools help in auditing the data captured by tags to ensure no unauthorized personal information is being inadequately safeguarded or improperly used, thereby aligning the data collection processes with GDPR, CCPA, or other relevant legal frameworks.

Additionally, the scope of debugging extends to the validation of data consistency. Often, tags are implemented across multiple pages and different versions of the same application. In such scenarios, ensuring consistency in data collection mechanisms across all channels is paramount. Debugging helps to ascertain that each tag adheres to the established data governance practices, thereby harmonizing the data across various touchpoints.

Lastly, debugging in tag management is crucial for ongoing maintenance. Digital landscapes are dynamic, with frequent updates to websites and applications that can inadvertently disrupt existing tags. Regular debugging sessions can preemptively catch issues arising from such updates, maintaining the fidelity of data collection practices.

In conclusion, debugging holds a multifaceted role in effective tag management. It ensures that tags are correctly implemented, optimizes their performance, guarantees compliance with data privacy laws, maintains consistency across multiple platforms, and supports ongoing maintenance. Through meticulous validation, diagnosis, optimization, and auditing, debugging fortifies the reliability and accuracy of the data collected, which in turn underpins informed decision-making and strategic planning. Without robust debugging practices, the integrity of the entire data ecosystem stands compromised, underlining its significance in the realm of tag management.

## 3.3 Overcoming Challenges in Tag Implementation

Implementing tags effectively across digital platforms is often met with a variety of challenges, each uniquely impactful on the overall success of the initiative. These challenges can range from technical barriers and resource limitations to alignment issues across different teams. Understanding these challenges in depth and developing strategies to overcome them can significantly enhance the efficiency and accuracy of tag implementation.

One of the primary challenges in tag implementation is the technical complexity involved. Tags often require precise coding and an understanding of both the platform and the specific requirements of the tag. This can be particularly cumbersome for organizations that lack in-house technical expertise. Without the right technical know-how, tags can be incorrectly placed or misconfigured, leading to inaccurate data collection and reporting. To overcome this challenge, it's crucial for organizations to invest in ongoing training for their technical staff or to work closely with experienced third-party vendors who specialize in tag management. Leveraging tag management systems (TMS) can also simplify the process by allowing non-technical users to manage tags through a user-friendly interface.

Another significant challenge is the inconsistency in tag deployment across various platforms. Tags need to be uniformly applied across all digital touchpoints to ensure cohesive data collection. However, ensuring this consistency often requires coordination across multiple teams and sometimes even across different departments. Miscommunication or misalignment between these groups can result in fragmented tag implementation, where some platforms have the correct tags while others do not. To address this, it's essential to establish clear communication channels and processes for tag deployment. Creating detailed documentation and guidelines for tag implementation can help standardize procedures across teams. Regular audits and reviews can also ensure that tags are consistently applied and maintained.

Resource limitations pose another barrier to effective tag implementation. Organizations, especially smaller ones, may struggle with allocating sufficient time, budget, and personnel to manage and oversee the tagging process. Staff members may be stretched thin with other responsibilities, leaving little bandwidth for meticulous tag implementation. To mitigate this, organizations should prioritize their tagging needs based on the business objectives and focus their resources on the most critical tags first. Partnering with outsourcing firms or adopting automated tagging solutions can alleviate some of the resource strain. Additionally, investing in scalable tagging infrastructure can provide long-term benefits and reduce the need for continual resource allocation.

Cybellium - Google Tag Manager Certification

Data privacy and compliance issues also create hurdles in tag implementation. With the advent of stringent data protection regulations like GDPR and CCPA, organizations must ensure that their tagging practices are compliant with these laws. Improperly implemented tags can inadvertently lead to data breaches or non-compliance, resulting in hefty fines and reputational damage. To avoid this, organizations need to work closely with their legal and compliance teams to understand the regulatory requirements of data collection and tagging. Implementing consent management platforms (CMP) can also help in ensuring that data collection is compliant by obtaining user consent before tags are fired.

Testing and validation of tags pose further challenges. Tag implementations need to be thoroughly tested to ensure they function correctly and capture the intended data. This often involves rigorous quality assurance (QA) processes, which can be time-consuming and require detailed expertise. Implementing a robust testing framework, which includes both automated and manual testing, can help in identifying issues early in the process. Tools like tag debuggers and validators can provide real-time insights into the functioning of tags, making it easier to pinpoint and rectify problems.

Lastly, the dynamic nature of digital environments can complicate tag implementation. Websites and applications are frequently updated, and these changes can inadvertently affect the tags. To overcome this, establishing a change management process that includes a review of tag placement as part of any update rollout can be highly effective. This ensures that any new changes do not disrupt the existing tag structure.

In conclusion, overcoming challenges in tag implementation requires a multi-faceted approach that includes investing in technical expertise, fostering inter-departmental communication, prioritizing resources, ensuring compliance, and adopting robust testing and change management processes. By proactively addressing these challenges, organizations can achieve accurate and efficient tag implementation, leading to better data collection and informed decision-making.

## 3.4 Adapting Tag Strategies to Different Marketing Goals

In the dynamic landscape of digital marketing, the effective use of tag strategies can be transformative, particularly when tailored to different marketing goals. Tags—be they meta tags, social media tags, or tracking tags—act as informational signposts and can significantly influence the direction and success of marketing campaigns. Below, we delve into the ways in which tag strategies can be adapted to serve a variety of marketing objectives.

To begin with, one crucial marketing goal is increasing website visibility in search engine results pages (SERPs). For this, Search Engine Optimization (SEO) tags such as title tags, meta descriptions, and header tags become essential. Title tags, for instance, should be adapted to include primary keywords and convey a clear, compelling message that prompts clicks. According to best practices, they should be no longer than 60 characters to avoid truncation in SERPs. Meta descriptions, while not a direct ranking factor, significantly affect click-through rates and must succinctly summarize the page content, ideally within 160 characters. Header tags (H1, H2, etc.) should be used hierarchically to structure content, making it easily digestible for both users and search engine crawlers.

For brands aiming to enhance their social media presence, social media tags like hashtags and mentions play a pivotal role. Hashtags can increase the reach of posts when used strategically. For instance, popular and trending hashtags can amplify visibility but should be balanced with more niche or branded hashtags to target a specific audience. Research by TrackMaven highlights that posts with 7-9 hashtags tend to achieve optimal engagement on platforms like Instagram. Mentions, on the other hand, can foster partnerships and collaborations. When a brand mentions another user or entity, it signals a relationship and can lead to reciprocal promotion. Crafting a strategy around when and whom to mention can therefore bolster community engagement and expand network reach.

Converting website visitors into leads is another common marketing objective, often achieved through the use of tracking tags or pixels. Tools like the Facebook Pixel or Google Analytics tags help marketers understand user behavior by tracking actions such as page views, sign-ups, and purchases. This data is invaluable for retargeting campaigns. For example, a visitor who abandoned a shopping cart can be retargeted with ads displaying the products they showed interest in. The specificity of these tracking tags allows for highly personalized marketing efforts, increasing the likelihood of conversion.

Another goal might be improving user engagement on the brand's website. Here, interactive tags such as schema markup can significantly enhance the user experience. Schema markup tags provide search engines with detailed information about the content on the webpage, which can lead to richer and more informative results for users. For example, a recipe page with schema markup might display cooking times, calorie counts, and user ratings directly in the search result, making the link more appealing to potential visitors. Implementing these tags can lead to higher click-through rates and longer site visits, directly contributing to improved user engagement metrics.

Brands focusing on content marketing can greatly benefit from tags that categorize and organize content effectively. Tags and categories applied to blog posts or video content can help in building content clusters, which not only aids SEO but also enhances user navigation. A well-structured tagging system allows users to easily find related content, increasing the time spent on the site and encouraging deeper exploration. Furthermore, content tags can be used to identify which topics resonate most with the audience, providing feedback that can guide future content creation.

Lastly, for companies prioritizing brand monitoring and reputation management, tags can be adapted to track mentions and sentiments. Tools such as Brandwatch or Mention use tags to filter out relevant mentions of the brand across the internet. By analyzing these tags, companies can quickly address negative comments or capitalize on positive publicity. Sentiment analysis tags help in understanding the general mood around the brand, allowing for more responsive and informed PR strategies.

In conclusion, adapting tag strategies to various marketing goals requires a nuanced understanding of both the tags themselves and the specific outcomes desired. Whether aiming to enhance visibility, boost social media engagement, convert leads, improve user interaction, optimize content marketing, or manage brand reputation, the careful and strategic application of tags can lead to measurable improvements and significant returns on marketing investments.

# 4. Google Tag Manager and Analytics Growth

Growth in digital marketing hinges on the effective use of data to make informed decisions. As businesses strive to refine their online presence and optimize their strategies, tools like Google Tag Manager and Google Analytics become invaluable assets. This chapter delves into the integration and utilization of these powerful resources to track, analyze, and ultimately drive growth.

Google Tag Manager simplifies the process of managing and deploying marketing tags (snippets of code) on your website without having to modify the site code directly. By centralizing tag management, it enables more agile marketing operations and quicker implementation of tracking codes that provide insights into user behavior.

Complementing Google Tag Manager, Google Analytics offers a robust platform for detailed data analysis. By capturing and presenting comprehensive metrics on web traffic, user interactions, and conversion patterns, it empowers businesses to make data-driven decisions. From understanding user demographics to tracing the customer journey, Analytics provides the actionable insights necessary for strategic growth.

Together, these tools contribute significantly to crafting a data-driven marketing strategy that can adapt to market changes and user preferences in real-time. As we explore their features and applications, you'll gain the knowledge needed to leverage them effectively, setting the stage for measurable and sustainable growth.

# 4.1 The Role of Tag Management in Enhancing Analytics

In the increasingly data-driven landscape of digital marketing, the effective use of analytics is critical for making informed business decisions. Central to this is the concept of tag management, which has emerged as a crucial tool for deploying, managing, and optimizing tags across various digital properties. Tag management systems (TMS) streamline the process of implementing and governing tags—snippets of code embedded in a website to collect data—without having to hard-code these elements directly into the site. This offers a suite of benefits that significantly enhance the scope, depth, and accuracy of analytics.

One of the core roles of tag management is the simplification of the tag deployment process. Traditionally, embedding tags directly into a website required significant coordination with IT departments, a process often mired in considerable delays and potential coding errors. With a TMS, marketers can easily add, modify, or remove tags through a user-friendly, web-based interface. This ease of deployment means that businesses can rapidly respond to new analytics needs, market changes, or campaign requirements. Consequently, the ability to expedite these changes leads to more timely and relevant data collection, optimizing analytical capabilities.

Beyond ease of deployment, tag management significantly enhances data governance and quality. Inconsistent or erroneous tag execution can lead to incomplete or inaccurate data, which, in turn, compromises decision-making processes. TMS platforms provide version control and debugging functionalities, allowing businesses to meticulously manage their tags and identify any issues before they affect data collection. Furthermore, many TMS solutions offer robust testing environments where tags can be vetted before they go live. This helps ensure that data quality is maintained, promoting more accurate, reliable analytics.

The role of tag management also extends to facilitating enhanced website performance. Poorly managed tags can lead to increased page load times, adversely impacting user experience and SEO rankings. A TMS consolidates and optimizes tag execution, reducing the strain on webpages and ensuring they load more efficiently. By doing so, it helps maintain a seamless user experience, which is imperative for both customer satisfaction and the overall efficacy of analytics. Faster page loads mean that visitor behaviors can be accurately tracked without the confounding variable of slow page performance skewing the data.

Another significant contribution of tag management to analytics is in enabling advanced data segmentation and personalization. Through a TMS, businesses can categorize and target tags to specific user groups, deriving more granular data insights. These segmented data points can then inform more tailored marketing strategies and personalization efforts. For instance, understanding the behavior of audience subgroups allows for more effective targeting of ad campaigns, email marketing efforts, and content delivery strategies. Consequently, the analytics derived from these segmented efforts provide more actionable insights that can lead to higher conversion rates and better user engagement.

Furthermore, tag management plays a critical role in enhancing cross-device and cross-channel analytics. In a multi-channel marketing ecosystem, the ability to track customer interactions across various touchpoints—desktop, mobile, email, social media, etc.—is vital. A TMS can manage and harmonize tags across these channels, ensuring cohesive data collection that provides a unified view of customer behavior. This holistic perspective is invaluable for comprehensive analytics, enabling businesses to understand the complete customer journey and optimize their strategies accordingly.

Finally, compliance and privacy concerns are increasingly paramount in the digital age. Regulations such as GDPR and CCPA necessitate stringent data governance practices. Tag management systems often include features to manage user consent and privacy settings, ensuring that data collection remains compliant with regulatory requirements. This reduces the risk of legal repercussions and enhances consumer trust by demonstrating a commitment to data privacy.

In summary, the role of tag management in enhancing analytics is multifaceted. It streamlines the deployment and management of tags, maintains data quality, improves website performance, enables advanced segmentation and personalization, facilitates cross-channel analytics, and ensures compliance with privacy regulations. By leveraging TMS platforms, businesses can dramatically elevate their analytical capabilities, driving more informed decision-making and bolstering overall marketing effectiveness. The integration of tag management into an analytics strategy is not just a technical convenience but a strategic necessity in today's competitive digital landscape.

## 4.2 Measuring the Impact of Tags on Data Accuracy

When examining the impact of tags on data accuracy, several dimensions must be considered, including the methodologies employed in tagging, the context and objectives of tagging, and the downstream implications for data processing and insights generation. This analysis is crucial for understanding how tags can enhance or compromise the integrity and utility of data.

Tags, in the context of data processing, serve as metadata that categorizes or labels data points to facilitate their identification, retrieval, and analysis. The precision in tagging directly influences the quality of insights extracted from the data. Proper tagging helps to ensure that data can be effectively organized and easily referenced, which, in turn, elevates the overall accuracy of data-driven decisions.

**Methodologies of Tagging**

Accurate tagging begins with the selection of an appropriate methodology. Methods can vary widely depending on the nature of the data and the system used for tagging. For static datasets, automated tagging algorithms—often based on predefined rules or machine learning techniques—can be employed. Specific guidelines must be adhered to when designing these algorithms to minimize errors and biases. For instance, a text-tagging algorithm might use natural language processing (NLP) to identify and label content-specific features such as sentiments, topics, or named entities.

Human-in-the-loop methods, where data tagging is performed manually or semi-manually by human operators, may complement automated systems, especially in handling ambiguous or complex cases that cannot be reliably resolved by algorithms alone. While manual tagging introduces a level of subjectivity and potential for human error, it often ensures higher fidelity in contexts that require nuanced understanding, such as tagging sentiment in qualitative text data.

**Context and Objectives**

The impact of tags on data accuracy also heavily relies on the context and objectives of tagging. For example, in e-commerce databases, tags might categorize products by attributes such as type, brand, or price range. Accuracy in such contexts is paramount because incorrect tags can lead to misdirected marketing efforts, poor customer experience, and erroneous sales analytics.

In a different context, such as scientific research databases, tags might indicate methodological details or research outcomes. Here, the rigor of tag assignment

Cybellium - Google Tag Manager Certification

affects the reproducibility of research findings and the quality of meta-analyses. The objectives of tagging in such a scenario are aligned with the principles of robust data practices, where accuracy is critical for advancing the scientific knowledge base.

## Implications for Data Processing

The impact of tagging on data accuracy is directly observed in downstream data processing tasks. Tags facilitate more efficient data retrieval and organization, making it possible to quickly assemble datasets that meet specific criteria. For instance, in a large dataset of customer feedback, accurate sentiment tags enable analysts to quickly filter and analyze positive or negative feedback without sifting through unorganized data.

In databases supporting machine learning models, tags are instrumental in training datasets. Incorrect tags can lead to mislabeled training data, ultimately distorting the model's learning process. This results in models that make inaccurate predictions, which can have severe consequences in applications such as medical diagnoses, financial forecasting, or autonomous driving.

Furthermore, properly tagged data enhances the precision of data integration efforts, where datasets from various sources are combined. Tags act as keys or descriptors that align and match data points from disparate datasets, ensuring consistency and coherence. Errors in tagging can lead to mismatches or duplication, compromising the integrity of the integrated dataset.

## Measuring Tag Accuracy

To quantify the impact of tags on data accuracy, several metrics and evaluation techniques can be employed. Precision and recall are commonly used metrics to assess tagging accuracy in classification tasks. Precision measures the proportion of correctly assigned tags out of all tags assigned, while recall measures the proportion of correctly assigned tags out of all relevant tags. F1 score, the harmonic mean of precision and recall, offers a balanced view of tagging performance.

Additionally, confusion matrices can provide insights into specific types of tagging errors, revealing patterns that can inform refinements in tagging methodologies. Using inter-annotator agreement metrics such as Cohen's Kappa can help understand the consistency of manual tagging efforts, shedding light on the reliability of human taggers.

In conclusion, the impact of tags on data accuracy permeates through multiple layers of data handling and processing. From the initial methodological choices to the varied contexts and objectives, and finally to their implications in data retrieval, machine learning, and data integration, every step underscores the significance of precise tagging. Evaluating and continually refining tagging practices through robust metrics is essential to maintaining the integrity and utility of data in any analytical framework.

## 4.3 Tags as a Competitive Advantage

In today's increasingly digital and interconnected world, businesses must leverage every possible advantage to stay ahead of their competition. One such powerful and often underutilized tool is tagging. Tags, or metadata labels, have evolved from simple organizational tools into critical components that can significantly impact a company's competitive advantage.

Firstly, tags enhance search engine optimization (SEO). By strategically incorporating tags into content, businesses can improve their search engine visibility. Tags help search engines understand the context and relevance of web pages, making it easier for users to find them. This increased visibility translates into more traffic, higher engagement, and better conversion rates. For example, a company in the food industry might use tags like "healthy recipes," "quick meals," or "vegetarian options" to attract specific user groups actively searching for those terms. The effective use of tags can elevate a business from obscurity to prominence in search engine results, ultimately drawing in more customers than competitors who neglect this tactic.

Moreover, tags can significantly optimize internal workflows and data management. In large organizations with vast amounts of data, tagging can streamline the process of organizing, retrieving, and analyzing information. By applying consistent and meaningful tags across datasets, employees can quickly locate the resources they need, thereby increasing efficiency and reducing wasted time. For instance, in an e-commerce setting, tagging products with attributes like "best-seller," "limited edition," or "on sale" enables faster stock management and prompts quicker decision-making. Enhanced efficiency translates to quicker responses to market changes, superior customer service, and ultimately, a stronger market position.

Another critical advantage of tags is their role in personalization. Tags allow businesses to tailor experiences to individual user preferences and behaviors. By tracking which tags are frequently associated with user interactions, companies can better understand customer interests and needs. For instance, a streaming service might use tags such as "action," "drama," or "documentary" to recommend content to users based on their viewing history. Personalized experiences foster customer loyalty, increase user engagement, and elevate the overall customer experience. Personalization powered by tags thus not only attracts customers but also retains them, giving businesses a significant competitive edge.

In the realm of social media and content marketing, tags are indispensable. Hashtags, a form of tagging, facilitate content discovery and engagement on platforms like Twitter, Instagram, and LinkedIn. By using trending or relevant hashtags, companies can widely disseminate their content to interested audiences. Additionally, tags can help in tracking the success of marketing campaigns. For instance, a company launching a new product might use a unique hashtag to monitor its reach and engagement in real-time. This real-time feedback allows for agile adjustments and fine-tuning of marketing strategies, ensuring that they remain effective and impactful.

In addition, tags can play a vital role in competitive intelligence. By monitoring the tags used by competitors in their content, marketing campaigns, and product offerings, businesses can gain valuable insights into industry trends and competitor strategies. This information can be used to benchmark performance, identify market gaps, and innovate new solutions. For instance, by noting that competitors are frequently using tags related to "sustainable products," a business might decide to highlight its own eco-friendly practices, thereby appealing to environmentally conscious consumers and differentiating itself in the marketplace.

Furthermore, tags can enhance collaboration within and outside the organization. Shared tagging systems enable different departments to work cohesively by standardizing how information is categorized and accessed. For example, a project management tool with robust tagging capabilities allows teams from marketing, sales, and product development to track project milestones, share resources, and align strategies seamlessly. Externally, collaborative tagging on shared platforms with partners or suppliers can streamline joint ventures and co-marketing efforts, driving mutual growth and strengthening market position.

In conclusion, tags are more than just simple organizational tools; they are strategic assets that can translate into significant competitive advantages. From enhancing SEO and personalizing customer experiences to optimizing workflows and facilitating marketing and intelligence efforts, tags underpin a broad spectrum of business activities. Companies that skillfully leverage tagging will not only improve their operational efficiency but also create more engaging, relevant, and adaptive customer experiences, thereby securing a robust position in their respective markets.

# 4.4 Case Studies of Growth-Driven Tag Strategies

Case Studies of Growth-Driven Tag Strategies

In a dynamic business environment, the evolution of digital marketing has fostered innovative methods for brands to reach and engage their audiences. Among these methods, growth-driven tag strategies have emerged as a powerful approach to track user interactions, optimize campaigns, and drive business growth. Through examining case studies, one can better understand how these strategies are effectively applied across various industries.

**Case Study 1: E-commerce**

An e-commerce company specializing in apparel leveraged growth-driven tag strategies to enhance user experience and increase conversion rates. By implementing advanced tagging on their website, the company tracked detailed user behavior such as time spent on product pages, items added to the cart, and abandoned carts.

Analyzing this data allowed the company to identify critical drop-off points in the purchasing process. For example, a significant number of users abandoned their carts after viewing the shipping costs. With this insight, the company tested various strategies, such as discounted shipping for first-time users and free shipping over a certain purchase threshold. These changes, spurred by data collected through tags, resulted in a 15% increase in conversion rates and a higher average order value.

Moreover, the company employed A/B testing to determine the most effective landing pages. Tags recorded user interactions on different versions of the page, providing quantifiable metrics on performance. By continuously optimizing the user journey based on the tagged data, the business maintained a competitive edge and sustained growth in a crowded marketplace.

**Case Study 2: Healthcare**

A healthcare provider utilized tag strategies to enhance patient engagement on their digital platforms. With the objective of improving appointment bookings and disseminating important health information, tags were set up to monitor user interactions with various sections of the website, from blog articles to appointment scheduling pages.

The data revealed that most visitors accessed health-related articles but did not proceed to book appointments. This insight led to a focused content strategy where articles about specific health concerns were linked to related services and appointment booking options. Additionally, tags monitored the effectiveness of call-to-action buttons, allowing the provider to refine their placement and wording for better engagement.

Success was measured through a significant uptick in appointment bookings, a reduction in bounce rates, and deeper insights into patient needs, which guided their content creation moving forward. This holistic use of tagging not only improved patient care but also established the provider as a trusted source of health information.

## Case Study 3: SaaS Company

A Software as a Service (SaaS) company applied growth-driven tag strategies to streamline its product onboarding process and enhance customer retention. Tags were used to track user activity within their software, from initial sign-up to feature usage and support interactions.

By analyzing tagged data, the company identified that users who did not engage with certain key features were more likely to cancel their subscriptions. This discovery prompted the introduction of guided onboarding tours and in-app tutorials that specifically highlighted these features. Tags tracked the completion rates of these tours and correlated them with long-term retention data, demonstrating that users who completed the onboarding were significantly more likely to remain active subscribers.

This data-driven approach also clarified the need for personalized support. Tags monitored common issues that arose during the onboarding process, leading to the development of a dedicated support team and a comprehensive FAQ section. The result was a notable decrease in churn rate and increased customer satisfaction, directly contributing to the company's growth.

## Case Study 4: Marketing Agency

A digital marketing agency aimed to improve the effectiveness of its client campaigns using growth-driven tag strategies. By implementing tags across client websites and marketing assets, the agency gathered extensive data on user interactions, campaign performance, and lead conversions.

For one client, a B2B technology firm, tags highlighted that their highest-quality leads were coming from specific blog posts rather than paid advertisements. Armed with this data, the agency shifted budget allocations towards content marketing and SEO strategies that promoted these high-performing articles.

The agency also used tags for real-time campaign adjustments. During a campaign, tags tracked engagement metrics across various channels, allowing the team to promptly reallocate resources to the highest-performing platforms. This responsive approach resulted in a 30% increase in lead generation compared to previous campaigns.

In conclusion, these case studies underscore the impact of growth-driven tag strategies in diverse sectors. By leveraging tagged data, businesses can optimize user experiences, improve customer engagement, and drive exponential growth. The iterative nature of tag-based insights allows for continuous improvement and adaptation in an ever-evolving digital landscape.

# 5. Strategic Planning for Tag Management

In today's digital landscape, the ability to effectively manage and deploy tags across websites and mobile applications is pivotal to capturing and analyzing user behavior. As organizations grapple with vast amounts of data streaming in from diverse touchpoints, a streamlined, strategic approach to tag management becomes crucial. This chapter delves into the intricate process of crafting a robust strategic plan for tag management, highlighting the essential components that ensure accuracy, efficiency, and scalability.

We begin by exploring the foundational principles of tag management, emphasizing why a strategic framework is indispensable for achieving seamless data integration and analytics. The importance of aligning tag management objectives with broader business goals is underscored, providing a context for the advanced strategies that follow.

Readers will gain insights into assessing current tagging infrastructures, identifying gaps, and prioritizing improvements. Best practices for collaboration between cross-functional teams, from marketing to IT, will be outlined, ensuring that all stakeholders are engaged in the planning process. Additionally, we will address common challenges faced in tag implementation and the strategic methodologies to overcome them, setting the stage for a more integrated and intelligent approach to data handling.

Prepare to uncover a wealth of knowledge that will empower your organization to treat tag management not merely as a technical necessity but as a strategic asset capable of delivering profound business insights and driving informed decision-making.

# 5.1 Developing a Comprehensive Tag Strategy

Developing a comprehensive tag strategy is a critical component for enhancing the discoverability and relevance of content in the digital landscape. Tags serve as metadata that help both search engines and users understand and navigate content more effectively. An effective tag strategy not only improves the user experience but also significantly impacts SEO performance and content management. Here are several key aspects to consider when developing a comprehensive tag strategy.

First and foremost, it's essential to conduct thorough keyword research. Understanding the terms and phrases that your target audience uses when searching for content similar to yours is crucial. Tools such as Google's Keyword Planner, Ahrefs, and SEMrush can provide valuable insights into the volume, competition, and relevance of various keywords. Once you have a list of potential tags, prioritize them based on their relevance to your content and their popularity among your target audience. This initial step ensures that the tags you choose are both specific to your content and aligned with user search behavior.

Another important aspect is consistency. Tags should be used uniformly across your content to create a coherent tagging system. Inconsistent use of tags can lead to fragmented data, making it difficult for users to find related content and for you to analyze the performance of your tags accurately. Establishing guidelines for tag usage can help maintain consistency. These guidelines should include rules on tag capitalization, singular vs. plural forms, and the appropriate length and number of tags per piece of content.

Additionally, it's vital to balance specificity and generality in your tags. Highly specific tags can target niche audiences more effectively, but overly specific tags might not attract significant search traffic. On the other hand, very general tags can drive higher traffic but might result in lower engagement due to a lack of relevance. Finding a middle ground by using a mix of broad and specific tags can help maximize both reach and relevance. For example, a blog post about "vegan recipes" might use specific tags like "vegan breakfast recipes" alongside broader tags like "healthy eating."

Monitoring and analyzing the performance of your tags is another critical component. Analytics tools can track how users interact with tagged content, providing insights into which tags are driving the most traffic and engagement. Regularly reviewing these metrics allows you to adjust your tag strategy in response to user behavior and trends. Tags that consistently underperform can be replaced or refined, while high-performing tags can be reused and expanded upon.

It's also important to consider the user experience when developing your tag strategy. Tags should be intuitive and useful from the user's perspective, making it easier for them to discover and navigate related content. Including tags that reflect common user queries and grouping related tags together can enhance the browsing experience. For instance, if you run an e-commerce site, tagging products with attributes like "summer collection," "organic material," and "best sellers" can help users quickly find what they're looking for.

Incorporating tags into your overall content strategy can also yield significant benefits. Tags can inform content creation by highlighting popular topics and gaps in your existing content. For instance, if tags related to a specific topic consistently drive high engagement, it may be worthwhile to produce more content in that area. Conversely, identifying underrepresented tags can reveal opportunities for content diversification.

Finally, it's worth noting that tag strategies should evolve over time. The digital landscape is dynamic, with user preferences and search engine algorithms continually changing. Regularly revisiting and updating your tag strategy ensures that it remains aligned with current trends and continues to meet user needs. Staying informed about industry developments and adapting your strategy accordingly will help maintain the effectiveness and relevance of your tags.

In summary, developing a comprehensive tag strategy involves thorough keyword research, maintaining consistency, balancing specificity and generality, monitoring performance, enhancing user experience, integrating tags with content strategy, and evolving with trends. By meticulously considering these aspects, you can create a robust tagging system that enhances content discoverability, improves SEO, and provides valuable insights for ongoing content development.

## 5.2 Aligning Tag Objectives with Marketing Goals

In the rapidly evolving landscape of digital marketing, the strategic alignment of tag objectives with overarching marketing goals is a critical factor for achieving success. Tags, which are snippets of code embedded within web pages, serve as the backbone for capturing essential data that marketers use to make informed decisions. Ensuring that these tags are aligned with marketing goals allows businesses to track performance metrics effectively, optimize campaigns, and ultimately drive greater return on investment (ROI).

The primary step in this alignment process is to delineate clear marketing goals. These goals can range from increasing brand awareness, driving website traffic, generating leads, or enhancing customer engagement to boosting sales conversions. Once these goals are defined, mapping them to specific tag objectives becomes a systematic and intuitive process.

For instance, consider a business that aims to increase brand awareness. The appropriate tag objectives could include tracking page views, monitoring the reach and engagement of content across social media platforms, and analyzing the performance of display ads. Implementing tags to capture this specific data provides valuable insights into how well the brand is resonating with its audience and allows for timely adjustments in marketing strategies.

Similarly, if the primary marketing goal is to generate leads, the focus shifts to capturing data related to form submissions, phone calls, and other conversions. Tags can be set up to track key events such as click-through rates on call-to-action buttons and forms filled out on landing pages. This data is instrumental in understanding how well the marketing funnels are performing and where potential leaks might be occurring. It also paves the way for A/B testing and other optimization techniques to improve lead generation efforts.

In e-commerce environments where boosting sales conversions is a top priority, aligning tag objectives entails tracking user behaviors that contribute to the purchase decision. This includes monitoring add-to-cart actions, checkout processes, and actual purchases. Enhanced e-commerce tagging features offered by platforms like Google Analytics provide detailed insights into what products are viewed the most, the average order value, and the customer's journey on the site. This granular level of tracking helps in identifying barriers to purchase and opportunities for upselling and cross-selling.

Engagement metrics are equally vital for businesses focused on enhancing customer interaction. Tags play a crucial role in capturing user engagement metrics such as time spent on site, scroll depth, video views, and interaction with interactive elements like surveys or quizzes. These metrics offer a window into the quality of user experience and help in fine-tuning content to make it more appealing and engaging.

Furthermore, the alignment of tag objectives with marketing goals is not a one-time effort but an ongoing process. It requires regular audits and updates to ensure that the tags are functioning correctly and capturing the data accurately. This iterative process allows for continuous improvement and adaptation to changes in marketing strategies or technological advancements.

Businesses must also ensure compliance with privacy regulations like GDPR and CCPA when setting up tags. This involves obtaining user consent for data collection and providing options for users to opt-out, thus maintaining transparency and trust.

In conclusion, the alignment of tag objectives with marketing goals is an indispensable component of a data-driven marketing strategy. By clearly defining marketing goals and mapping them to precise tag objectives, businesses can unlock actionable insights, optimize their marketing efforts, and achieve desired outcomes. This convergence of data and strategy not only enhances the efficiency of marketing operations but also contributes to sustainable business growth.

# 5.3 Strategic Execution of Tag Implementation

Implementing tags strategically is a vital aspect of contemporary digital marketing and data analytics. By embedding snippets of JavaScript into websites, tags collect a myriad of user interactions, ultimately allowing businesses to track and analyze behaviors to optimize both user experience and business strategies. Effective tag implementation, however, demands meticulous planning and execution due to its complexity and variety of potential impacts, ranging from website performance to data governance.

To start, a comprehensive tagging strategy begins with defining clear objectives. Without well-established goals, tags could gather irrelevant data, leading to misinformation or data overload. Typically, objectives align with broader business goals such as increasing conversion rates, improving visitor segmentation, or enhancing user experience. By determining specific aims from the outset, one can ensure that every tag serves a purpose and contributes to actionable insights.

Next, it is essential to create a detailed tagging plan. This involves mapping out where each tag will be placed, what data it will collect, and how that data will be used. Often, this process starts with devising an implementation framework that includes an overview of the website's structure. For example, different tags may be required for product pages than for blog posts or landing pages, and a thorough understanding of these distinctions enables more precise tracking.

Documentation is another critical element. Replete with detailed instructions and standardized naming conventions, robust documentation facilitates consistent implementation across teams and departments. Developers, marketers, and analysts must be on the same page to prevent discrepancies that could skew data. Clear documentation also serves as a reference for future updates or troubleshooting, ensuring sustainable tag management.

Selecting the right tools for tag management is equally crucial. Tag Management Systems (TMS) like Google Tag Manager, Adobe Launch, or Tealium IQ house all tags in a single repository, permitting easier updates and minimizing the risk of errors. With a TMS, new tags can be added without altering the website's codebase, expediting deployment and adjustment processes. Moreover, these systems frequently offer debugging and version control, adding layers of reliability and accuracy to tag deployment.

Furthermore, careful consideration must be given to the tag's impact on site performance. Tags, especially poorly optimized ones, can slow down web pages, causing user frustration and potential loss of business. As modern consumers

Cybellium - Google Tag Manager Certification

expect speedy browsing experiences, balancing comprehensive data collection with minimal performance degradation becomes a tightrope walk. Techniques such as asynchronous loading, where tags load independently of the main content, can mitigate such issues, ensuring that analytics do not come at the cost of user satisfaction.

Security and privacy considerations also play predominant roles. With growing concerns around data protection and privacy regulations like GDPR or CCPA, businesses must ensure that their tag management complies with legal standards. This often involves anonymizing data and obtaining clear consent from users before tracking begins. Failure to comply not only risks legal ramifications but also damages brand reputation.

Periodic auditing of tags is another step in strategic tag implementation. Over time, marketing campaigns evolve, and website architectures change, necessitating regular review of tag performance and relevance. Audits ensure that tags are functioning correctly, collecting the right data, and not duplicating or redundantly gathering information. They also identify and eliminate "orphaned" tags—those inadvertently left behind by outdated or removed tools and platforms—which can clutter analytics and confuse data interpretation.

Continuous optimization based on insights gleaned from the collected data forms the final component of strategic tag implementation. Real-time data allows businesses to quickly pivot or adjust strategies to better meet user needs. However, this requires a solid framework for analyzing the incoming data. Techniques such as funnel analysis, cohort analysis, and user journey mapping can bring valuable insights, provided the underlying tagging structure is correctly implemented and maintained.

In conclusion, strategic execution of tag implementation is a multifaceted endeavor requiring careful planning, ongoing management, and continuous optimization. By aligning tagging initiatives with business objectives, utilizing robust tools, ensuring legal compliance, and iteratively refining the approach, businesses can harness the full potential of their web analytics to drive informed decision-making and achieve sustained growth.

## 5.4 Adapting Tag Strategies During Platform Changes

The dynamic nature of digital platforms necessitates constant vigilance and adaptability. As social media platforms and search engines evolve, so too must the strategies employed to navigate them effectively. One critical aspect of this navigation is the intelligent use of tags. The inherent fluidity of platform algorithms, user behaviors, and interface modifications presents both challenges and opportunities for content creators, marketers, and businesses alike.

Tags, fundamentally, are metadata elements that help in organizing and categorizing content, making it easily discoverable by users. They serve as pivotal tools in enhancing visibility and searchability. However, as platforms institute algorithm updates and design changes, the efficacy of existing tag strategies may diminish. Therefore, the ability to adapt tag strategies in response to these transitions is imperative.

Firstly, it is essential to stay informed about platform updates. Platforms like Instagram, YouTube, and Twitter frequently announce changes via official blogs, developer notes, or social media updates. Staying abreast of these updates allows for proactive rather than reactive adjustments. For instance, when Instagram shifted its focus from chronological to algorithmic feed, the way users interacted with tags and how content surfaced changed dramatically. Creighton (2020) notes that understanding such shifts can aid in recalibrating tag strategies to align with new engagement paradigms.

Understanding user behavior is another cornerstone. Platforms change, but user behavior often changes more slowly. User data analytics can provide insights into which tags continue to drive engagement and which do not. Tools like Google Analytics, Hootsuite Insights, or platform-specific analytics dashboards can provide crucial data. By examining metrics such as click-through rates, impressions, and interactions, one can identify the tags that remain effective despite platform alterations. For instance, a decline in engagement metrics post-update may signal the need to revise tagging practices.

The use of evergreen tags versus trend-specific tags is a strategic decision. Evergreen tags are those generally broad and consistently relevant, while trend-specific tags are timely and linked to current events or popular topics. During platform changes, an over-reliance on trend-specific tags can be risky due to their ephemeral nature. Conversely, evergreen tags may provide a stable foundation. Simultaneously, monitoring emerging trends and swiftly associating them with relevant content can capture timely engagement. Balancing these types of tags can provide resilience against fluctuating platform dynamics.

Optimizing tag hierarchies is another adaptive strategy. Hierarchies involve structuring tags in a way that follows a logical progression from broad to specific. For instance, on YouTube, overarching categories followed by specific keywords can help in capturing a broad audience initially while still catering to niche searches. When platforms undergo changes, revisiting these hierarchies to ensure they align with new indexing or categorization methodologies can sustain or even enhance visibility.

Testing and iteration are integral to adaptation. A/B testing different tag combinations and analyzing performance can provide empirical data on what works best in the new platform context. For example, experimenting with variations of tags on a piece of content and measuring which versions generate more engagement can offer actionable insights.

Collaboration with platform representatives or joining communities of practice can offer additional support. Engaging with forums, professional groups, or even directly with platform support can yield insider tips or best practices emerging across the industry. Communities such as the YouTube Creator Academy or Facebook's Business Groups provide opportunities to learn from peers' experiences and adapt strategies accordingly.

Lastly, it is important to maintain flexibility and foresight. While current platform changes may necessitate immediate adjustments, anticipating future trends and preparing for subsequent changes can provide a strategic edge. For example, artificial intelligence and machine learning advancements are increasingly influencing platform algorithms. Understanding these technologies and predicting how they might impact tagging can position one to adapt swiftly and effectively.

In conclusion, adapting tag strategies during platform changes is a multifaceted process that demands ongoing education, user behavior analysis, strategic experimentation, and community engagement. The rapidly evolving digital landscape offers both challenges and opportunities, and those who remain flexible and informed are most likely to thrive.

# 6. Best Practices for Tag Configuration

As digital ecosystems evolve, the ways we tag and categorize information have become both increasingly complex and crucial for operational success. Proper tag configuration is not just a technicality but a cornerstone of effective data management, allowing businesses to extract meaningful insights, drive engagement, and enhance user experience. This chapter delves into the essential strategies, methodologies, and tools that constitute best practices for tag management. By adhering to these principles, organizations can ensure their tagging framework supports seamless data retrieval, accurate reporting, and optimally targeted marketing initiatives. Whether you are a seasoned data analyst or a newcomer, understanding these best practices will empower you to maximize the efficiency and effectiveness of your tagging systems.

# 6.1 Setting Up Effective Tracking Tags

To set up effective tracking tags, it is crucial to understand their value in monitoring user behavior, gauging the performance of marketing campaigns, and driving data-informed decisions. Detailed and systematic tracking is the backbone of any successful digital marketing strategy as it allows for the meticulous observation of customer interactions and conversions. Here's a thorough step-by-step approach to planning, deploying, and managing tracking tags effectively.

The first and fundamental step in setting up effective tracking tags involves meticulous planning. Organizations should identify key metrics that align with their business objectives. This includes conversion rates, click-through rates, user engagement, and other vital KPIs. Once these critical metrics are identified, the next step is to decide which tagging solution best fits the organization's needs. Popular options include Google Tag Manager, Adobe Launch, and Tealium. Each comes with its own set of pros and cons, so choosing the right tool involves balancing functionality, ease of use, and integration capabilities with existing systems.

After selecting an appropriate tag manager, the process begins with creating a tagging plan. This comprehensive document should outline tags to be implemented, detailing their purpose, associated metrics, and their placement across the website or application. A well-organized tagging plan not only enhances efficiency but also simplifies maintenance and future updates. The tagging plan document serves as a reference point for all stakeholders involved and ensures consistency, completeness, and precision in tracking implementation.

With a tagging plan in place, configuring the tag manager follows. Typically, this configuration involves setting up a container within the chosen platform. A container is a code snippet provided by the tag management system, which must be embedded in the website's source code, usually in the header or footer sections. This container acts as a vessel for all subsequent tracking tags, enabling centralized management through the tag manager's dashboard. Once embedded, it facilitates seamless activation, modification, and deactivation of tags without further code changes, significantly improving agility and reducing dependency on development teams.

The actual creation of tracking tags comes next. For effective deployment, each tag must be meticulously customized to capture the precise information identified in the planning phase. Tags can range from basic pageview tags, which track user visits to specific pages, to more advanced event tags, capturing user interactions such as button clicks, form submissions, or product purchases. For instance, in Google Tag Manager, setting up a new tag involves selecting a tag type, configuring tag details, and defining triggers. Triggers are specific criteria that determine when the tag should fire, such as a particular page load or a custom event.

Testing and validation are pivotal. Even the most carefully planned and configured tags can encounter issues, leading to inaccurate data collection. Therefore, utilizing preview modes and debugging tools available in most tag management systems is crucial. These tools allow visualization of when and how tags fire, ensuring they behave as expected before going live. For example, Google Tag Manager's Preview Mode provides a simulated environment showing real-time tag activity, helping to verify if they are firing under the correct conditions.

It's also beneficial to implement tag sequencing and dependencies when dealing with multiple tags. Tag sequencing ensures that certain tags trigger in a specific order, which can be critical for tags that rely on previous data. For example, an ecommerce site might need to ensure that a transaction tag fires only after both the purchase and user session tags have fired correctly.

Once all tags are thoroughly tested and validated, the final step is to publish the container. This action pushes all the configured tags live, making them operational on the website or application. Continuously monitoring tag performance post-deployment is also essential. Regular audits help identify discrepancies or data quality issues, ensuring sustained accuracy and reliability of the collected data.

In summary, setting up effective tracking tags involves a structured approach encompassing thorough planning, precise configuration, rigorous testing, and ongoing monitoring. By following these steps, organizations can achieve robust data tracking that provides valuable insights into user behaviors, drives informed decisions, and ultimately enhances the effectiveness of their marketing strategies.

## 6.2 The Role of Custom HTML and JavaScript in Tag Management

Tag management systems (TMS) have become essential tools for digital marketing and web analytics, allowing organizations to efficiently manage and deploy tags across their websites without needing extensive coding expertise. Among the various functionalities offered by TMS, the integration of custom HTML and JavaScript plays a pivotal role in extending the capabilities and adaptability of these systems. This section delves into the importance and application of custom HTML and JavaScript in tag management, illustrating how these features provide enhanced control and customization.

At its core, tag management seeks to simplify the process of implementing and maintaining tags. Tags are snippets of code that collect data or perform specific functions, such as tracking user behavior, integrating third-party services, or triggering marketing campaigns. While most TMS platforms offer a repository of pre-built tags for common use cases, the inclusion of custom HTML and JavaScript allows for unparalleled flexibility and customization.

Custom HTML and JavaScript fill the gaps left by pre-configured tags. There are numerous scenarios where an out-of-the-box solution may not adequately meet the specific needs of a business. For instance, a company might want to track a unique user interaction that isn't covered by standard tags, or they might integrate a third-party service that doesn't have a pre-built tag available in the TMS library. In such cases, custom code becomes indispensable. By incorporating custom HTML and JavaScript, businesses can create bespoke tracking mechanisms or integrations, tailored precisely to their requirements.

One significant advantage of using custom HTML and JavaScript in a TMS is agility. Traditional workflows would often require involvement from web developers for every new tag or tracking requirement. This process could become time-consuming and bottleneck critical marketing initiatives. However, with the ability to directly insert custom code into the TMS, marketing teams can implement and adjust tags on the fly, without waiting for developer resources. This results in quicker deployment of tags, immediate troubleshooting, and timely optimizations based on data insights.

Security and reliability are other crucial considerations when utilizing custom HTML and JavaScript. Tags executed on a webpage have the potential to manipulate content, access sensitive data, or impact page performance. Thus, organizations must implement rigorous validation and testing procedures to ensure that custom code does not introduce vulnerabilities or degrade the user experience. Many TMS platforms offer sandbox environments and debugging tools to test custom HTML and JavaScript code in a controlled setting, allowing for safe experimentation before live deployment.

In addition to flexibility and agility, custom HTML and JavaScript also enable a higher degree of sophistication in tracking and analytics. For example, businesses can write custom code to capture complex user interactions, such as multi-step form submissions, video engagement, or in-page navigation behaviors, and funnel these data points into analytics platforms for deeper insights. Advanced use cases might include dynamically altering tags based on the user's contextual data, integrating machine learning models for real-time decision-making, or automating personalized content delivery.

Furthermore, by leveraging custom HTML and JavaScript, organizations can ensure a consistent and unified tagging strategy across multiple digital channels. This is particularly valuable for large enterprises with sprawling digital ecosystems, as it facilitates standardized data collection practices and reduces the risks associated with disparate tagging methods. Consequently, this standardization can lead to enhanced data accuracy, which in turn underpins more informed and strategic decision-making processes.

Moreover, the role of custom HTML and JavaScript in tag management extends to testing and optimization. A/B testing, multivariate testing, and personalization efforts often require conditional tag firing based on specific criteria or user attributes. Custom scripts can be crafted to achieve such granular control, ensuring that tags only activate under defined conditions, leading to more effective experiments and targeted user experiences.

In summary, the incorporation of custom HTML and JavaScript within tag management systems significantly amplifies the potential and utility of these platforms. By providing flexibility, allowing for quicker execution, enhancing tracking capabilities, ensuring consistent data practices, and enabling sophisticated testing, custom code in a TMS environment is an indispensable asset. Organizations that master the use of custom HTML and JavaScript within their tag management processes are well-positioned to achieve a higher degree of precision and efficacy in their digital marketing and analytics efforts.

## 6.3 Managing Tags Across Multiple Platforms

In the digital age, managing tags across multiple platforms is an essential skill for businesses and content creators alike. Tag management involves the systematic organization and uniformity of metadata tags, which are crucial for categorizing content, enhancing discoverability, and improving user experience on diverse platforms such as websites, social media, and content management systems. Efficient tag management not only aids in better search engine optimization (SEO) but also ensures consistency and coherence across various digital environments.

One of the primary challenges in managing tags across multiple platforms is maintaining uniformity. Different platforms often have their own unique requirements and capabilities for tags, which can lead to inconsistencies if not managed properly. For instance, hashtags on social media might be used to boost engagement and discoverability, while metadata tags on a website are primarily intended for search engines. Consequently, creating a tagging strategy that accommodates the specific needs of each platform while maintaining a cohesive overarching structure is paramount.

Centralized tag management tools can be extremely beneficial in this regard. These tools serve as a hub where tags can be created, edited, and synchronized across various platforms. By centralizing tag management, businesses can ensure that all tags are consistent and up to date, thus avoiding the pitfalls of fragmented or outdated tagging policies. Tools like Google Tag Manager (GTM) simplify the process by allowing users to manage and deploy marketing tags without the need to alter the code on websites or apps constantly. This streamlines workflows and reduces the margin for error.

Another vital aspect to consider is the analysis and refinement of tags over time. Effective tag management is not a one-time task but a continuous process that requires regular audits and updates. Analytics platforms can provide insights into how tags are performing, which tags are driving traffic, and which are underutilized. By analyzing these metrics, businesses can refine their tagging strategy to enhance performance further. For example, if certain tags are not yielding the expected traffic, it may be necessary to revisit the keywords associated with those tags or to implement better-targeted tags.

The importance of a well-defined tagging taxonomy cannot be overstated. A tagging taxonomy is essentially a framework or hierarchy that organizes tags systematically. Defining a clear taxonomy helps avoid redundancy and ensures that tags are both meaningful and relevant. This can involve creating categories and subcategories, differentiating between synonyms, and ensuring that tags are user-focused. For instance, a comprehensive tagging taxonomy for an e-commerce site might include categories like product type, brand, price range, and customer ratings. Each piece of content would then be tagged according to this predefined structure, ensuring consistency and easing navigation for both users and search engines.

Collaboration among different teams within an organization is also crucial for effective tag management. Since different teams might be responsible for various platforms—such as the web development team for the website and the social media team for social channels—coordination is key to maintaining consistency in application. Regular meetings and the creation of standardized guidelines can help ensure every team member is on the same page regarding tagging strategies and practices. This collaboration can prevent miscommunication and the disparate use of tags that could potentially confuse users or diminish the effectiveness of SEO efforts.

Addressing the technical nuances of each platform is another significant consideration. Each platform may have different constraints, whether it's character limits for tags, specific syntax requirements, or varying degrees of support for certain metadata. Understanding these nuances and adapting the tag management strategy accordingly is essential. For instance, while Twitter might limit hashtags to a concise number of characters, platforms like YouTube allow extensive use of tags within video descriptions, requiring a more detailed focus on long-tail keywords.

Finally, emerging trends and technologies, such as artificial intelligence (AI) and machine learning (ML), offer innovative ways to enhance tag management. AI can automate tag generation based on content analysis, predicting which tags will be most effective in driving engagement and visibility. This not only saves time but also increases the accuracy and relevance of tags, allowing for a more dynamic and responsive tag management strategy.

In summary, managing tags across multiple platforms is a complex but crucial task involving maintaining uniformity, leveraging centralized tools, conducting regular audits, defining a clear taxonomy, fostering team collaboration, addressing platform-specific nuances, and incorporating advanced technologies. By adhering to these principles, businesses can significantly improve their content management capabilities and enhance user engagement across various digital landscapes.

## 6.4 Tools and Techniques for Optimizing Tag Performance

In the realm of digital marketing, optimizing tag performance is pivotal for ensuring the efficiency and effectiveness of tracking, monitoring, and analyzing user interactions. Tags, essentially snippets of code embedded within webpages, facilitate a wide range of functionalities including tracking user behavior, enabling retargeting, and integrating third-party services. As marketers and developers strive to enhance tag performance, they can leverage a diverse array of tools and techniques designed to streamline this process.

One foundational tool for tag optimization is the tag management system (TMS). Examples of TMS include Google Tag Manager, Adobe Launch, and Tealium IQ. A TMS provides a centralized platform from which all tags can be managed, enabling users to oversee, deploy, and modify tags without needing to manually adjust the underlying code on each webpage. This centralization not only reduces the potential for errors but also speeds up the process of implementing new tags. Additionally, TMS platforms often include features that allow for the conditional triggering of tags, ensuring they only fire when specific criteria are met, thereby optimizing page load times and conserving bandwidth.

Testing and validating tags is another critical technique for optimizing performance. Tools like Google Tag Assistant and Adobe Debugger allow users to verify whether tags are firing correctly and retrieve comprehensive diagnostics about tag implementation. These tools can be used to identify errors or misconfigurations that may obstruct the accurate collection of data. By regularly utilizing such validation tools, marketers can ensure that their tags remain functional and aligned with their tracking objectives.

Speed and performance analysis is integral to the optimization process. A variety of tools, such as Lighthouse, WebPageTest, and GTmetrix, can analyze the impact of tags on page load times. Tags that excessively delay page rendering negatively affect user experience and search engine rankings. By evaluating metrics such as time to first byte (TTFB), total blocking time, and cumulative layout shift, these tools help identify tags that may need optimization or removal. After diagnosing these issues, optimizing tags might involve minifying code, asynchronously loading tags, or deploying them through a content delivery network (CDN) to improve loading speed.

Leveraging first-party data where feasible is another effective strategy. Dependence on third-party tags can introduce performance bottlenecks and privacy concerns. By shifting towards first-party data collection methods, organizations can mitigate these issues. This approach not only enhances tag performance but also aligns with increasingly stringent data protection regulations.

A/B testing and analytics platforms, like Google Optimize or Optimizely, can further refine the performance of tags. These platforms allow for the testing of different tag configurations and placements to determine their impact on user behavior and webpage performance. By experimenting with variations and analyzing the resultant data, marketers can make informed decisions about which tag implementations yield the best results.

Moreover, employing server-side tagging presents an advanced optimization technique. Unlike traditional client-side tagging, server-side tagging processes tag requests on the server rather than in the user's browser. This approach reduces the amount of JavaScript loaded on the client side, leading to faster page loads and improved data security. Popular solutions, such as Google Tag Manager Server-Side, offer streamlined pathways to integrate this method into existing infrastructures.

Monitoring tag performance through continuous audit and review rounds off the optimization process. Dedicated monitoring tools like ObservePoint can routinely audit tags across web properties, ensuring ongoing compliance, performance, and security. Regular audits help identify any anomalies or deviations from expected behavior, allowing for timely adjustments and maintenance.

In summary, optimizing tag performance is a multifaceted endeavor that necessitates the utilization of diverse tools and techniques aimed at achieving a balance between efficient data collection and optimal webpage performance. Through the strategic implementation of tag management systems, validation tools, speed analysis, first-party data strategies, A/B testing platforms, server-side tagging, and continuous monitoring, organizations can significantly enhance the performance and reliability of their tagging infrastructure, thereby driving better insights and outcomes from their digital marketing efforts.

# 7. Debugging and Troubleshooting Tags

Debugging and troubleshooting are critical skills for anyone working with complex systems, and this is especially true when dealing with tags in software development. Tags, whether in programming languages, markup languages, or version control systems, are essential for organizing, managing, and navigating your codebase or content. However, they can also introduce a unique set of challenges when things go wrong.

In this chapter, we dive into the nuances of debugging and troubleshooting tags. We will explore common issues that can arise, ranging from syntax errors to more insidious logical mistakes that can disrupt the functionality of your applications. This discussion will equip you with practical strategies and tools to diagnose and fix problems efficiently. By the end of this chapter, you will have a robust understanding of how to approach issues with tags methodically, ensuring smoother and more reliable operations in your projects.

# 7.1 Enhancing Debugging Skills with Preview Mode

Debugging is an indispensable skill in the toolkit of any developer, offering a pathway to identify, diagnose, and rectify code anomalies that can lead to system failures or unexpected behavior. In recent years, the introduction of Preview Mode in various integrated development environments (IDEs) has revolutionized the debugging process, providing developers with more efficient and intuitive methods to tackle code issues.

Preview Mode, often referred to as live previews or real-time previews, allows developers to see the immediate effect of their code changes without needing to resort to lengthy rebuilds or manual refreshes. By providing an interactive environment where modifications are instantly reflected, Preview Mode enables a more dynamic and responsive debugging process. This not only boosts the efficiency of error detection but also significantly reduces the time required to implement and verify fixes.

A critical benefit of using Preview Mode is the ability to observe the real-time execution of code. Traditional debugging methods often involve setting breakpoints, stepping through code, and inspecting variables at different stages of execution. While these techniques are effective, they can sometimes be cumbersome and time-consuming. Preview Mode simplifies this process by allowing developers to see live updates and outputs directly as they code. For instance, in web development, making a change to the HTML or CSS can immediately show the visual result in the browser. This instantaneous feedback loop enables developers to quickly identify and correct issues, such as layout problems or incorrect styling, without needing to repeatedly toggle between the code editor and the browser.

Moreover, Preview Mode enhances the debugging process by providing a more holistic view of the application's state. Developers can see not just the end result of their code but also how different pieces of the application interact in real-time. This is particularly beneficial in complex systems where issues may arise from the interplay between various components. By observing the live interactions, developers can gain deeper insights into where and why certain problems occur, making it easier to pinpoint and address root causes.

Another significant advantage is improved collaboration and code reviews. When working in teams, conveying the exact nature of a bug or the impact of a particular piece of code can be challenging. Preview Mode aids in this by offering a shared, live environment where team members can collectively observe and analyze the behavior of the application. This collaborative aspect fosters better communication and facilitates more effective peer reviews, as colleagues can see the live effects of suggested changes and provide immediate feedback.

In addition to real-time visual feedback, developers can leverage Preview Mode for performance monitoring and optimization. Tools integrated into Preview Mode environments often include capabilities for tracking memory usage, CPU load, and network activity in real-time. By observing these metrics as the code runs, developers can quickly identify areas where performance may be lagging and take proactive steps to optimize their applications. This proactive approach to performance debugging can lead to more efficient and responsive applications, ultimately improving the end-user experience.

However, relying solely on Preview Mode is not without its risks. One potential drawback is that the real-time feedback loop might obscure the broader implications of certain changes. Developers might be tempted to focus on immediate visual feedback rather than considering the long-term maintainability and scalability of their code. Therefore, while Preview Mode is a powerful tool, it should be used in conjunction with other debugging techniques and best practices to ensure robust and sustainable code development.

Another aspect to consider is the computational overhead associated with Preview Mode, especially in resource-constrained environments. Real-time previews can consume significant system resources, potentially slowing down the development process if the environment is not adequately equipped to handle it. Developers need to balance the convenience of instant feedback with the actual performance capabilities of their systems to maintain an efficient workflow.

In conclusion, Preview Mode represents a substantial leap forward in debugging methodologies, offering developers a more dynamic, interactive, and efficient way to identify and resolve issues within their codebase. By enabling real-time observation and interaction, it not only accelerates the debugging process but also enhances collaborative efforts and performance monitoring. Nonetheless, it is crucial for developers to integrate Preview Mode into a broader suite of debugging practices to fully harness its potential while mitigating any associated risks.

## 7.2 The Importance of Error Handling in Tag Deployment

Error handling in tag deployment is a pivotal consideration in the realm of digital marketing and analytics strategies. In an increasingly data-driven world, the deployment of tags across digital properties such as websites and mobile applications holds immense importance for tracking user behavior, monitoring performance, and optimizing marketing campaigns. However, the very process of deploying these tags can be fraught with potential errors that, if left unchecked, can negatively impact data accuracy, website performance, and ultimately, business outcomes. Thus, robust error handling mechanisms become indispensable.

At its core, the primary objective of error handling in tag deployment is to ensure data integrity. Tags, which are small snippets of code, serve to collect and relay data to various analytics tools and platforms. Any error in the tagging process can result in inaccurate data capture, leading to flawed analytics and misguided decision-making. For instance, a misconfigured tag might fail to send event data about a user's interaction with a website, causing gaps in tracking key metrics such as click-through rates, conversion rates, and user engagement levels. Effective error handling protocols detect, diagnose, and rectify such issues, ensuring that the data collected is both accurate and reliable.

Moreover, error handling is essential for maintaining the functional performance of digital properties. Tags are executed alongside the primary content of web pages and mobile applications. Erroneous tags can degrade the performance of these platforms by increasing page load times, causing rendering issues, or even leading to complete page failures. For example, a non-optimized tag that blocks the main thread can delay the loading of essential elements on a webpage, leading to a poor user experience and higher bounce rates. Implementing error handling ensures that tags are executed correctly and do not interfere with the core functionality of the site or app.

The process of error handling can be divided into several crucial steps: detection, diagnosis, mitigation, and monitoring. Detection involves identifying when and where errors occur during tag deployment. This can be achieved through automated tools and scripts that continuously scan for issues in real time. Diagnosis follows, wherein the root cause of the error is pinpointed. This step often requires the involvement of both the marketing and development teams, who must analyze error logs, test different scenarios, and debug the code to understand why the tag is malfunctioning.

Once the cause is identified, mitigation comes into play. Mitigation involves resolving the error and preventing it from reoccurring. This might involve correcting syntax errors, updating tag configurations, or even redesigning the tagging architecture to be more resilient to errors. Lastly, ongoing monitoring ensures that any future errors are swiftly detected and addressed. Monitoring involves setting up alerts and dashboards that provide real-time visibility into the status of deployed tags, enabling teams to respond proactively to any issues.

Furthermore, standardized error handling practices contribute to better collaboration and communication within an organization. When errors are logged and documented consistently, it creates a repository of knowledge that team members can refer to, facilitating faster resolution of similar issues in the future. This collective intelligence strengthens the organizational capacity to maintain high-quality data and operational efficiency.

In addition, the importance of error handling extends to compliance and privacy considerations. Many tags are responsible for collecting user data which must be handled in compliance with regulations such as GDPR or CCPA. Errors in tag deployment can lead to improper data collection methods that may violate these regulations, exposing the organization to legal risks and reputational damage. Effective error handling ensures that data collection practices are adhered to as per regulatory standards.

In conclusion, error handling is not merely an ancillary aspect of tag deployment but a fundamental necessity for ensuring the accuracy, performance, collaboration, and compliance of digital analytics endeavors. By meticulously implementing detection, diagnosis, mitigation, and monitoring protocols, organizations can safeguard the integrity of their data, enhance user experience, foster internal collaboration, and comply with regulatory requirements, thereby driving more informed and effective decision-making.

# 7.3 Managing Common Tag Errors and Solutions

Proper utilization of tags is crucial in any document, especially when dealing with HTML, XML, or similar markup languages. Whether you are a seasoned web developer, a novice to coding, or work on data representation formats, managing common tag errors and their solutions is an essential skill. Here we discuss several types of tagging errors and offer practical solutions to address them efficiently.

### Missing or Unclosed Tags

One of the most frequent errors encountered in markup languages is missing or unclosed tags. These errors can lead to improper rendering of web pages or documents, making them unusable or visually incorrect.

### Solution:

To counteract this, it is vital to use a reliable text editor or Integrated Development Environment (IDE) that highlights unclosed tags. Manual checking is also advised. Always ensure every opening tag has a corresponding closing tag. Automated validation tools or online validators can also help identify such issues by comparing opening and closing tags to ensure they match properly.

### Mismatched Tags

Mismatched tags can occur when an open tag is not closed with the corresponding closing tag — for example, opening a `<div>` tag and mistakenly closing it with `</span>`.

### Solution:

Consistently use the correct closing tag for every open tag. Utilizing tree-structured representations of your code can aid visually in spotting and correcting mismatched tags. Additionally, many modern code editors come with auto-completion features that suggest the correct closing tag automatically.

### Improper Nesting of Tags

When tags are nested improperly, such as placing a block-level element inside an inline level element improperly, it can result in rendering issues and non-conformance to web standards.

### Solution:

Cybellium - Google Tag Manager Certification

Understand the HTML specifications regarding which tags can be nested within others. Validate your documents using W3C validators to check for improper nesting. Auto-formatting tools within good text editors can also help reformat the tags to ensure proper nesting.

### Typographical Errors in Tags

Typographical errors can range from misspelling a tag name to incorrectly typing an attribute within a tag. These mistakes can break the functionality of your code or pages.

### Solution:

Using an editor with syntax highlighting can make typographical errors easier to spot. Version control systems can also help track changes and identify newly introduced errors by comparing versions of the document. Running your files through a linting process can catch errors that might otherwise be overlooked.

### Redundant or Unnecessary Tags

Sometimes, developers include redundant or unnecessary tags in their documents, which can bloat the file and slow down rendering without providing any functional benefit.

### Solution:

Perform regular audits of your code to remove any unnecessary or redundant tags. These can often be identified by analyzing the structure and seeing which tags do not contribute to the final outcome. Minifiers and code analysis tools can further assist by flagging sections of the code that may be simplified.

### Incorrect Attribute Usage

Using attributes incorrectly, such as placing attributes that are not supposed to be within a tag or misspelling attribute names, can compromise functionality and styling.

### Solution:

Refer to official documentation and guidelines for each tag to ensure attributes are used correctly. Many modern IDEs offer attribute suggestions and warnings when the incorrect attributes are used. Validating your document against a schema can also catch such errors.

## Incomplete Tag Syntax

Incomplete tag syntax, such as forgetting to close a tag properly with a '>', can break the structure of your document and cause rendering issues.

### Solution:

Syntax highlighting in code editors can immediately flag incomplete tags. Additionally, many editors have built-in tools that will automatically close tags for you once you start typing them. Employing a pre-commit hook that runs a syntax checker can prevent such errors from being committed to your version control system.

### Concluding Thoughts:

Learning to manage common tag errors is a fundamental skill for anyone working with markup languages. By utilizing efficient tools, adhering to best practices, and employing automated validators, you can significantly reduce the occurrence of these errors and streamline your development process. Regular updates to your knowledge base, alongside frequent code reviews and practices like pair programming, can also enhance error detection and resolution.

# 7.4 Case Studies of Effective Debugging Practices

Debugging is a critical skill in the software development process, and understanding effective practices can drastically improve the quality and reliability of the software. Case studies offer real-world examples that highlight the processes, tools, and techniques used by successful developers to troubleshoot and resolve issues. This section dives into several case studies that illustrate effective debugging practices, shedding light on the methods that have proven successful in various scenarios.

**Case Study 1: Debugging a Memory Leak in a Web Application**

In a high-traffic web application, users began experiencing slow performance, and resource utilization on the server was reaching dangerously high levels, leading to crashes. A memory leak was suspected. The development team initiated a systematic debugging process using several tools and methodologies.

**1. Identifying the Problem:** The first step was confirming the memory leak. The team monitored server metrics and used tools like HeapDump and VisualVM to observe memory usage over time. The consistent increase in memory consumption confirmed their suspicion.

**2. Isolating the Cause:** To narrow down the cause, the team segmented the application and tested individual components. Unit tests and load tests isolated the module responsible for the leak.

**3. Deep Dive with Profilers:** Tools such as JProfiler and YourKit were employed to profile the faulty module. These tools offered insights into object creation and helped identify objects that were not being garbage collected.

**4. Fixing the Issue:** After identifying incorrectly managed cached objects, the developers updated the caching mechanism to ensure proper invalidation and garbage collection.

**5. Verification and Deployment:** Before deploying the fix to production, the team thoroughly tested the application in a staging environment. Monitoring tools confirmed normalized memory usage, resolving the issue.

**Case Study 2: Debugging a Race Condition in a Concurrent System**

Concurrency issues can be particularly challenging to debug due to their non-deterministic nature. In this instance, a finance application encountered occasional incorrect transaction processing due to a race condition.

**1. Reproducing the Issue:** The first step was crafting a reproducible test case to study the issue. The developers used stress testing and simulating real-world scenarios to trigger the race condition.

**2. Logging and Tracing:** Enhanced logging was implemented to track the sequence of events leading up to the problem. Trace logs provided a timeline of thread interactions, revealing the timing discrepancies responsible for the race condition.

**3. Static Analysis and Code Review:** Static analysis tools like FindBugs and SonarQube helped in spotting potential threading issues. Additionally, a thorough code review uncovered improper synchronization practices.

**4. Implementing a Solution:** The team refactored the code to use proper synchronization mechanisms like locks and atomic variables, ensuring thread-safe operations.

**5. Testing and Production Rollout:** The solution underwent rigorous multi-threading testing to verify the fix. Once stable, it was deployed, and the application's transaction processing became reliable.

**Case Study 3:** Debugging Performance Bottlenecks in a Database-Driven Application

A retail application faced performance bottlenecks during peak shopping seasons, impacting user experience. The challenge was to identify and optimize the slow components within a complex database-driven system.

**1. Profiling the Application:** The team used application performance management (APM) tools such as New Relic and Dynatrace to profile the system, pinpointing slow database queries and high-latency API calls.

**2. Analyzing Slow Queries:** Database profiling tools like MySQL Profiler and Explain Plan helped analyze slow queries. Inefficient joins, missing indexes, and suboptimal query structures were identified.

**3. Optimizing Queries:** The developers revised the SQL queries, added necessary indexes, and denormalized certain tables to improve query efficiency. Queries with heavy load were separated and optimized individually.

**4. Performance Testing:** The optimized system underwent load testing using tools like Apache JMeter to simulate peak load. The tests confirmed significant performance improvements.

**5. Continuous Monitoring Post-Deployment:** After deploying the optimized code, continuous monitoring ensured that performance metrics aligned with expectations, and prompt action could be taken if new bottlenecks appeared.

**Conclusion**

These case studies provide valuable insights into effective debugging practices across various scenarios. Critical steps include identifying the problem, isolating its cause, employing the right tools, implementing and verifying solutions, and continuous monitoring. By studying these examples, developers can hone their debugging skills, leading to faster resolution of issues and more robust software systems.

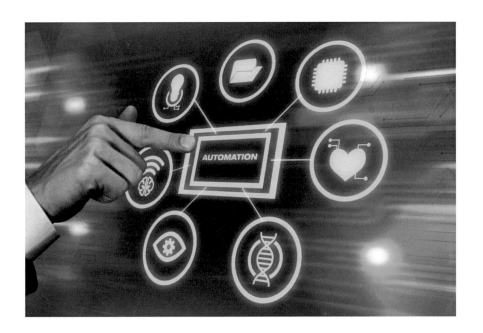

# 8. The Role of Automation in Tag Management

In the modern digital landscape, businesses constantly strive to harness the power of data to optimize their marketing strategies and improve user experiences. One crucial element in this equation is tag management, a process that enables the efficient collection, organization, and utilization of data from various digital touchpoints. With the increasing complexity and volume of data, manual tag management has become a daunting and often error-prone task.

Enter automation—a technological advancement that promises to revolutionize how organizations handle their tags. Automation in tag management is not merely a matter of convenience; it is a strategic necessity. By automating repetitive and time-consuming tasks, businesses can ensure accuracy, boost efficiency, and free up valuable resources that can be redirected towards more strategic initiatives.

This chapter delves into the transformative impact of automation on tag management. We will explore the tools and technologies that facilitate automated tag management, discuss best practices for implementation, and provide real-world examples that illustrate the tangible benefits. Through understanding the role of automation, organizations can better navigate the complexities of the digital age, ensuring they remain agile and competitive in an ever-evolving market.

# 8.1 Leveraging Automation Tools for Tag Deployment

In the digital age, the efficacy of online marketing campaigns increasingly hinges on the sophisticated deployment of tags. Tags—bits of code embedded on websites—serve a myriad of functions, from tracking visitor behavior to integrating with third-party services. Traditional manual tagging, though effective, is inherently labor-intensive and error-prone. Consequently, automation tools for tag deployment have emerged as indispensable assets. These tools streamline the process, ensure accuracy, foster scalability, and enable a more agile response to evolving marketing needs.

The sheer volume and variety of tags required for comprehensive website analytics and marketing can be overwhelming. These tags can range from simple Google Analytics tracking codes to complex remarketing pixels and A/B testing scripts. Individually coding and deploying these tags not only demands significant time and technical expertise but also increases the risk of human error. A single misplaced tag can lead to faulty data collection, which in turn can skew marketing insights and undermine campaign efforts.

Automation tools mitigate these challenges by centralizing and simplifying tag management. Tag Management Systems (TMS) like Google Tag Manager, Adobe Dynamic Tag Management, and Tealium iQ are among the most recognized solutions. These tools provide a user-friendly interface that allows marketers and analysts to deploy and manage tags without requiring extensive coding knowledge. Through a centralized dashboard, users can add, edit, and publish tags across their websites with minimal effort.

One of the key advantages of utilizing automation tools for tag deployment is the enhancement of accuracy. These systems standardize the tag implementation process, significantly reducing the potential for manual errors. Built-in validation and debugging features help identify and rectify configuration issues before tags go live, ensuring that data collection is both accurate and consistent. This precision in tag deployment translates directly into more reliable analytics, empowering marketers to make better-informed decisions.

Moreover, automation tools offer unparalleled scalability. As businesses grow and online presences expand, the need for a flexible and scalable tag management approach becomes critical. Automation tools can effortlessly handle the addition of new tags for emerging platforms, adapt to website redesigns, and accommodate increases in web traffic. This scalability ensures that businesses can continuously optimize their digital marketing strategies without being bogged down by technical constraints.

Another significant benefit of leveraging automation tools is the agility they provide. Digital marketing is an ever-evolving field, requiring rapid adaptation to new trends, technologies, and consumer behaviors. With manual tagging, making frequent updates or overhauls can be cumbersome and slow. In contrast, automation tools allow for swift tag modifications and deployments, enabling businesses to respond promptly to market changes and capitalize on new opportunities. For instance, launching a last-minute promotional campaign becomes more feasible when tags can be quickly adjusted to track specific metrics relevant to that campaign.

Furthermore, many automation tools come with advanced features that can enhance tag deployment and provide deeper insights. For instance, some tools offer tag firing rules and triggers that ensure tags are only activated under specific conditions. This targeted approach can improve website performance by reducing unnecessary data collection and conserving resources. Additionally, features like version control and change history allow teams to track and revert changes, fostering better collaboration and oversight.

Importantly, automation tools contribute to data governance and compliance. In an era where data privacy regulations, such as GDPR and CCPA, are of paramount concern, ensuring that tracking practices are compliant is critical. Automation tools can facilitate compliance by providing functionalities to manage consent and data privacy preferences, ensuring that tags are activated only when user permissions are granted. This reduces the risk of legal repercussions and builds consumer trust.

In conclusion, the deployment of automation tools for tag management significantly enhances the accuracy, scalability, agility, and compliance of digital marketing efforts. By centralizing and simplifying the tag implementation process, these tools not only mitigate risks associated with manual tagging but also empower marketers to make data-driven decisions swiftly and effectively. As digital landscapes continue to evolve, the role of automation tools in tag deployment will likely become even more critical, ensuring that businesses can maintain robust, insightful, and compliant online marketing practices.

## 8.2 The Impact of Automated Tagging Systems

Automated tagging systems have revolutionized the landscape of digital information management, dramatically altering how data is processed, categorized, and retrieved. These systems utilize sophisticated algorithms, often powered by artificial intelligence (AI) and machine learning (ML) technologies, to assign metadata to various types of content. This transformation has significant implications across multiple domains, including data management, business operations, and user experience.

One of the most profound impacts of automated tagging systems is in the realm of data management. In an age where data is produced at an unprecedented rate, the ability to efficiently organize and retrieve information is crucial. Automated tagging systems can process vast amounts of unstructured data, such as text, images, and videos, and classify them accurately in real-time. This capability not only alleviates the burden on human labor but also improves accuracy, as these systems reduce manual errors that could occur during data tagging.

Moreover, businesses across various industries benefit significantly from implementing automated tagging systems. In marketing, for instance, these systems can analyze consumer behaviors, preferences, and interactions to generate insights that drive targeted advertising campaigns. By automatically tagging user-generated content and behavior, companies can create more personalized marketing strategies, enhancing user engagement and conversion rates. In e-commerce, tagging systems enable more refined product categorization, which enhances the searchability of items and thereby increases sales.

In the field of content management, platforms such as social media and news organizations leverage automated tagging to enhance user experience and content discoverability. For example, tagging systems can automatically identify topics, keywords, or entities within articles or posts, facilitating better organization and easier access to related content. This not only improves the user experience by making content more relevant and accessible but also assists organizations in managing vast libraries of information without incurring high labor costs.

The impact of automated tagging extends to the legal and healthcare sectors as well. In legal domains, automated tagging systems can swiftly categorize case files, legal documents, and evidence, enabling quicker retrieval of pertinent information and thus accelerating legal processes. Healthcare industries leverage these systems to manage patient records, medical images, and research data efficiently. By accurately tagging patient information and medical documentation, healthcare providers improve data accessibility and ensure compliance with regulations, ultimately enhancing patient care and operational efficiency

Additionally, automated tagging systems have proven essential in enhancing digital security and surveillance. These systems can process and analyze video footage or audio recordings to detect and tag specific activities or anomalies, thereby enhancing monitoring capabilities. This application is particularly valuable in security-sensitive environments such as airports, banks, and military installations, where prompt detection of suspicious activities is critical.

Despite their numerous advantages, automated tagging systems are not without challenges. One significant concern is the potential for bias in AI and ML algorithms. If the training data used to develop these systems is biased, the resulting tags may be similarly skewed, leading to ethical and accuracy issues. For instance, in content tagging scenarios, biased algorithms might prioritize certain types of content over others, potentially marginalizing specific groups or viewpoints.

Furthermore, the reliance on automated systems may raise concerns about job displacement for roles traditionally involving data management and categorization. As organizations increasingly adopt these systems, the demand for manual data tagging may diminish, posing risks to employment in certain sectors. However, this also opens opportunities for upskilling and transitioning the workforce towards more complex roles that involve managing and improving these systems.

In summary, automated tagging systems have profoundly impacted various sectors by enhancing data organization, improving operational efficiency, and elevating user experiences. These systems harness the power of AI and ML to manage vast amounts of data, making information more accessible and actionable. While challenges such as bias and job displacement exist, the ongoing development and ethical application of these systems promise to further unlock their potential, driving innovation and efficiency across multiple fields.

## 8.3 Using APIs and Scripts Effectively in Tag Management

Effective utilization of APIs and scripts within the context of tag management is fundamental for enhancing the functionality and efficiency of digital marketing efforts. This process involves strategically leveraging Application Programming Interfaces (APIs) and custom scripts to streamline the deployment and management of tags on websites or mobile applications, thus enhancing data collection, analysis, and overall digital tracking practices.

APIs play a crucial role by allowing different software applications to communicate with each other. In tag management, APIs can be employed to automate various aspects of tag deployment and data retrieval. For instance, integrating third-party analytics tools through their APIs enables seamless data exchange, ensuring that relevant tracking information is consistently updated without manual intervention. This not only saves time but also minimizes human errors, ensuring accurate data collection.

One prominent example of utilizing APIs in tag management is the Google Tag Manager API. This powerful tool provides capabilities such as creating and configuring Google Tag Manager containers, managing tags, triggers, and variables, and even deploying changes across multiple environments. By using scripts to interact with the Google Tag Manager API, businesses can automate many repetitive tasks, such as bulk updating URLs for tags across numerous pages, adding new elements to tracking configurations, or even generating custom reports. This level of automation significantly boosts operational efficiency.

Beyond APIs, custom scripts offer another potent method for enhancing tag management. Scripts can be utilized to inject custom JavaScript into web pages to capture additional data that standard tags may not track by default. For example, a custom script can be used to track user interactions with complex website elements like sliders, pop-ups, or dynamically loaded content. This detailed level of user interaction tracking provides invaluable insights that can inform marketing strategies and improve user experience.

Moreover, custom scripts in tag management platforms, like Google Tag Manager, can facilitate advanced data manipulation. Suppose there is a need to modify certain data points before they are sent to analytics tools. In that case, custom JavaScript variables can be defined to format, sanitize, or transform data on the fly. This flexibility ensures that the data collected aligns perfectly with the analytical goals, providing clear, actionable insights.

Security is another crucial consideration when using APIs and scripts in tag management. Access tokens or API keys should be securely managed and restricted to the minimum necessary permissions to avoid unauthorized access. Scripts, on the other hand, should be thoroughly tested and reviewed to prevent vulnerabilities such as cross-site scripting (XSS) attacks that could compromise the site's security and user data. Embedding best practices for API security and scripting hygiene into the processes can mitigate risks and maintain the integrity of the data management system.

Furthermore, collaboration between development and marketing teams is essential for success. Developers can create robust API integrations and custom scripts, while marketers can specify the events and data points critical for their analysis. This cooperation ensures that the tagging setup is both technically sound and tailored to meet marketing objectives.

Lastly, continuous monitoring and optimization are vital. APIs and scripts should be regularly reviewed to ensure they are functioning as intended and capturing the needed data. Computational logs and analytics dashboards can offer real-time insights into tag performance, helping to identify and rectify any discrepancies swiftly. Iterative testing and refinement ensure that the tag management system evolves alongside the changing digital landscape and emerging business requirements.

In conclusion, APIs and scripts are powerful tools in the arsenal of tag management, enabling automated efficiency, enhanced data accuracy, and comprehensive tracking capabilities. By fostering collaboration, ensuring security, and committing to continuous optimization, businesses can leverage these technologies to gain deep insights, inform strategic decisions, and ultimately enhance their digital marketing effectiveness.

## 8.4 The Future of Automation in Tag Management

The landscape of digital marketing is continually evolving, and one area that has experienced significant advancements is tag management. Tag management systems (TMS) have streamlined the process by which businesses implement and manage their digital marketing tags, providing a more efficient and organized way to handle these vital components. One of the most exciting developments on the horizon for tag management is the increasing integration of automation. As we look toward the future, the automation in tag management promises to bring about several transformative changes.

Firstly, automation in tag management will enhance accuracy and reduce human error. Tags are snippets of code that track various metrics and behaviors on a website, and even minor mistakes in deploying these tags can lead to inaccurate data collection, which in turn affects marketing decisions. By automating the deployment and management of these tags, businesses can ensure greater precision. Automated systems can follow pre-set rules and protocols, ensuring that tags are placed correctly and consistently. This consistency is crucial because it ensures that the data collected is reliable, forming a solid foundation for analytics and decision-making.

Secondly, automation will significantly expedite the deployment process. Traditionally, implementing new tags or making changes to existing ones required manual intervention, often involving coordination between marketing and IT departments. This could cause delays and slow the pace of marketing campaigns. With automation, the process can be accelerated. Marketing teams can use intuitive interfaces to set up automation rules that automatically implement the required tags, thus reducing the dependency on IT staff and speeding up the implementation time. Faster deployment means that marketing strategies can adapt more swiftly to changing market conditions, giving businesses a competitive edge.

Additionally, automation in tag management will facilitate better compliance and governance. With increasing regulations around data privacy and consumer protection, businesses need to ensure that their tag management practices comply with laws such as GDPR or CCPA. Manual tag management makes it difficult to consistently adhere to these regulations across all tags and campaigns. Automated systems, however, can be programmed to enforce compliance rules consistently, ensuring that all deployed tags are in line with legal requirements. This not only helps in avoiding legal pitfalls but also builds consumer trust by demonstrating a commitment to data privacy and protection.

Moreover, the future of automation in tag management will likely leverage artificial intelligence (AI) and machine learning (ML) to further refine and optimize tag deployment. AI algorithms can analyze vast amounts of data to identify patterns and trends that would be difficult for humans to discern. By integrating AI with tag management systems, these platforms can make more informed decisions about when and how to deploy tags for maximum effectiveness. For example, AI could dynamically adjust tags in real-time based on user behavior to optimize marketing campaigns' performance continuously.

Integration with other marketing technologies will also be a significant aspect of automation in tag management. Modern marketing stacks comprise various tools and platforms for customer relationship management (CRM), email marketing, social media management, and more. Automated tag management systems will become more interoperable, seamlessly working in conjunction with these other tools. This will create a more cohesive digital marketing ecosystem where data flows smoothly between systems, enabling more sophisticated analytics and more effective marketing strategies.

Simplicity and accessibility will also improve with automation in tag management. As the technology becomes more advanced, user interfaces will likely become more intuitive, making it easier for non-technical marketing professionals to implement and manage tags. This democratization of tag management will empower marketers to take greater control over their campaigns without needing deep technical knowledge.

Ultimately, the future of automation in tag management is about creating a more efficient, accurate, and compliant system for managing digital marketing tags. By reducing human error, speeding up deployment, ensuring compliance, leveraging AI, integrating with other technologies, and enhancing accessibility, automation will transform tag management into a more powerful and indispensable tool for digital marketers. As these advancements continue to unfold, businesses that embrace automated tag management will be better positioned to adapt to the rapidly changing digital landscape, drive more effective marketing campaigns, and achieve their growth objectives.

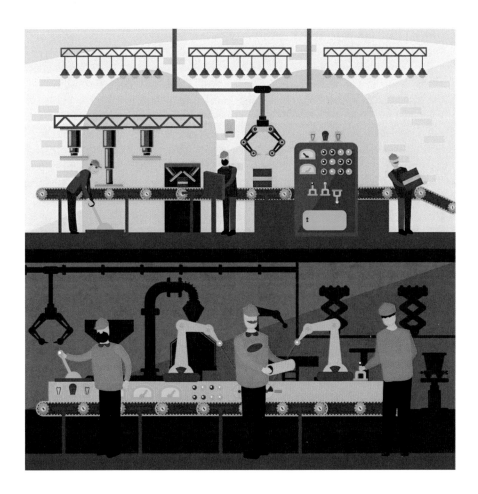

# 9. Tag Management in Different Industries

As the digital landscape continues to evolve, the complexities of managing and optimizing data have become increasingly nuanced. The importance of efficient tag management cannot be overstated, as it plays a pivotal role in data collection, analysis, and the overall performance of digital operations. Different industries, with their unique set of challenges and opportunities, require tailored approaches to effectively manage their tagging systems. This chapter delves into the intricacies of tag management across various sectors, exploring industry-specific strategies, best practices, and case studies that illustrate successful implementations. By understanding the distinctive needs and solutions applicable to each industry, businesses can leverage tag management to enhance their digital strategies and achieve optimal results.

# 9.1 Tag Strategies in E-commerce

Tag strategies in e-commerce have become critical in optimizing both the browsing and shopping experience for consumers. As e-commerce platforms grow more sophisticated, the need for effective tag strategies has increased, helping businesses enhance navigation, improve search engine optimization (SEO), and provide personalized shopping experiences. This section delves into some of the most essential strategies for applying tags effectively in e-commerce settings.

One of the most important aspects of tag strategy is the use of keywords. Keywords are fundamental in aligning the products with the search queries of potential buyers. When used correctly, they can significantly improve visibility on search engines. Tools like Google Keyword Planner or Moz can assist in identifying high-impact keywords related to the products being sold. By implementing these keywords appropriately, on both product pages and meta descriptions, businesses can improve their search rankings and attract more organic traffic.

Another critical strategy involves the use of descriptive tags. Descriptive tags go beyond basic keywords to provide additional context and specificity. For example, instead of tagging a shoe simply as "sport shoes," descriptive tags like "running shoes," "trail running shoes," or "marathon shoes" can be employed. These tags not only help customers find exactly what they're looking for more efficiently but also improve the website's internal search engine accuracy. This precision is important for converting searches into sales, which is the ultimate goal.

User-generated tags, often in the form of reviews and comments, also play a significant role in e-commerce. Allowing customers to tag products with their own descriptions can enrich the content and provide insights into how consumers perceive the products. These user-generated tags can often reveal emerging trends or unexpected uses of a product, which businesses can then leverage for marketing and inventory decisions. Moreover, user-generated tags tend to foster greater engagement and create a sense of community around the brand.

Semantic tagging is another powerful strategy that has gained traction. This involves using tags not just as labels but as connectors to a specific context or meaning. Semantic tags help in creating a richer, more intuitive user experience. For example, if a consumer is looking for "organic baby shampoo," semantic tagging can ensure that related products also surface, such as "organic baby lotion" or "organic baby soap." This interconnectedness makes the shopping experience more seamless and can significantly increase the average order value.

Category-based tagging should also not be overlooked. By tagging products by categories, e-commerce platforms can offer better-organized and more navigable avenues for consumers. Categories can be broad, like "Men's Clothing" or narrow, like "Slim Fit Jeans." Effective category-based tagging allows consumers to easily filter through available options and quickly find what they're looking for. This efficiency is crucial for reducing bounce rates and improving overall user satisfaction.

Another dimension to consider is seasonal and event-based tagging. Products can be tagged for specific times of the year, such as "Christmas gifts," "Back-to-School," or "Black Friday Deals." Event-based tags align perfectly with marketing campaigns and can drive significant traffic during peak shopping periods. Businesses can use tools like Google Trends to anticipate the right timing for these seasonal tags to maximize their effectiveness.

Analytics-driven tagging involves the use of data analytics to refine and optimize tag usage. By analyzing which tags are attracting the most traffic and converting into sales, businesses can hone their tagging strategies for better results. Tools like Google Analytics allow for in-depth monitoring and provide insights that can be translated into actionable strategies. Understanding tag performance ensures that the tags in use are always relevant and effective.

Moreover, personalizing tags based on customer behavior can make a significant difference. Dynamic tagging adjusts the tags shown to users based on their past behavior, purchases, and browsing history. This personalized approach ensures that the most relevant products are always presented to the user, increasing the likelihood of conversion. Personalized tagging mirrors the in-store experience where knowledgeable staff might recommend items based on a shopper's interest.

In summary, a well-constructed tag strategy is indispensable for the success of an e-commerce business. By incorporating keyword optimization, descriptive tagging, user-generated tags, semantic tagging, category-based tagging, seasonal/event-based tagging, analytics-driven tagging, and personalized tags, businesses can significantly enhance their search engine performance, improve the user experience, and ultimately drive higher sales. Adopting these multifaceted tag strategies allows e-commerce platforms to stay competitive in an increasingly crowded marketplace.

## 9.2 Tag Management in the Service Industry

In today's rapid digital transformation, managing the vast array of data tags efficiently and effectively has become pivotal for success in the service industry. Tags, which are snippets of code placed on a website, allow businesses to collect data on visitor interactions and behavior, driving critical insights for making informed decisions. The process of tag management has therefore emerged as a vital competency, aiming to streamline the deployment, handling, and analysis of these tags within digital properties.

Tag management in the service industry extends beyond the mere technicalities of embedding tags. It encompasses a strategic framework that integrates with the organization's marketing, sales, and customer service operations. One primary reason for deploying a tag management system (TMS) is to improve the agility and precision of data collection without necessitating constant IT interventions. This agility is crucial, particularly in the service industry where customer interactions and preferences shift rapidly, and timely data can inform quick pivots in strategy.

A robust TMS offers real-time control and visibility over all tags, reducing redundancy and ensuring that each tag serves its intended purpose efficiently. By minimizing the loading time of websites through optimized tag deployment, businesses in the service industry enhance user experience – a critical factor in retaining customers and improving service delivery.

Furthermore, a TMS enables the seamless integration of third-party tools and server-side tagging, ensuring that data flows smoothly across different platforms such as Customer Relationship Management (CRM) systems, marketing automation tools, and analytics platforms. This integrated ecosystem of tools allows service providers to build a holistic view of customer interactions, thus refining service delivery and tailoring personalized experiences.

Compliance with regulations such as GDPR and CCPA also underscores the importance of sophisticated tag management. With growing concerns over data privacy, the ability to manage and audit tags ensures that customer data is collected and processed ethically and legally. A TMS facilitates easier compliance through features that allow businesses to manage consent and automate the anonymization of personal data.

Tag management also significantly impacts marketing efficacy within the service industry. Tags that track user behavior and engagement can feed into real-time analytics, allowing marketers to measure campaign performance more accurately and optimize ad spend. This granularity in data ensures that marketing efforts are both cost-effective and highly targeted, driving better ROI and improving customer acquisition and retention rates.

The implementation of a TMS involves several key steps. First, it is crucial to conduct a tag audit to identify all active tags and review their necessity and performance. This audit helps to remove redundant or obsolete tags, thereby reducing clutter and potential site slowdowns. Next, businesses should establish a governance policy which defines how tags should be implemented, tested, and maintained, ensuring uniformity and precision across the board.

Training and collaboration across departments are also essential. Oftentimes, different teams within a service organization—be it marketing, IT, or customer service—interact with tags. Ensuring cross-functional teams are trained on the TMS fosters better tag governance and smoother operations.

In addition, the adoption of a robust TMS involves continuous monitoring and optimization. Tags and their requirements evolve, and so must the strategies for their management. Regular reviews and adaptations to the TMS are necessary to ensure that the system remains aligned with the company's goals and current digital landscape.

Overall, effective tag management in the service industry is not just a technical requisite but a strategic enabler. By harnessing a comprehensive TMS, service providers can capture and interpret crucial customer data with precision, adapt to regulatory demands proficiently, and enhance overall marketing and operational effectiveness. Such managerial acumen is indispensable in today's service-oriented economy, where data-driven insights shape the trajectory of customer satisfaction and business success.

## 9.3 Managing Tags in Technology and Innovation

Tags are an invaluable asset in effectively managing technology and fostering innovation. They serve as a mechanism to categorize, prioritize, and streamline information, making it accessible and functional. Proper tag management is paramount for businesses striving to maintain a competitive edge, particularly in an era where vast amounts of data are generated daily. Understanding the principles and best practices in managing tags can provide a structured approach to navigating complex technological landscapes and fostering an environment conducive to innovation.

The primary function of tags is to sort and filter information, but their role extends beyond simple classification. Tags enable efficient data retrieval, allowing for swift access to essential information. This becomes increasingly important as organizations grow and the volume of data expands. In technology and innovation contexts, tags can be applied to anything from coding repositories, project files, research documents, and even physical assets, ensuring that relevant parties can locate and utilize the necessary resources without unnecessary delay.

In software development, tags are used within code repositories to mark different versions of codebases. This practice, often associated with version control systems such as Git, allows developers to manage different iterations of their projects seamlessly. For instance, a version of software tagged as 'v1.0' would signify a specific stable release, while 'v1.1-beta' might denote a beta version in development. Such tagging aids in the efficient coordination of development efforts, tracking progress, and maintaining overall organization within the project lifecycle.

Tags also play a crucial role in project management. Software tools like JIRA, Asana, and Trello utilize tags to organize tasks, assign priorities, and track the progress of various elements within projects. By applying tags like 'urgent,' 'in-progress,' or 'completed,' project managers can easily monitor the status and ensure that essential tasks are given the attention they require. This streamlined approach not only heightens efficiency but also enhances the team's ability to respond to changes and challenges quickly, thereby fostering an agile and innovative working environment.

In research and development (R&D), tags facilitate the management and categorization of vast quantities of information. Researchers often face the daunting task of sifting through published papers, experimental data, and patent filings. By meticulously tagging these resources, researchers can create a structured repository of knowledge. This structure enables swift retrieval of pertinent information, whether for literature reviews or to inspire new innovations. Tags like 'nanotechnology,' 'machine learning,' or 'sustainable energy' help in pinpointing relevant studies or prior work, expediting the ideation processes.

Effective tag management involves establishing naming conventions and hierarchies, ensuring consistency and clarity across the organization. Developing a standardized tagging system requires collaboration and consensus among team members, aligning tags with the organization's goals and workflows. Regular audits and updates are also necessary to adapt the tagging system to evolving needs and technological advancements.

Moreover, the integration of automated tagging systems powered by machine learning and artificial intelligence can significantly enhance tag management. These systems can analyze content and suggest appropriate tags based on predefined criteria or previous tagging patterns. Automation reduces the manual burden on employees and increases the accuracy and consistency of tags, leading to more reliable data management.

Security and privacy concerns are also integral to tag management. Tags should be used with caution to avoid disclosing sensitive information inadvertently. Implementing access controls and encryption can mitigate such risks, ensuring that only authorized personnel can view or modify certain tags, particularly in environments that handle confidential data.

In conclusion, tags are a critical tool for managing technology and innovation. They facilitate organization, enhance efficiency, and promote agility within teams and projects. By employing best practices in tag management, such as standardization, automation, and security measures, organizations can harness the full potential of tags. This structured approach supports the seamless integration of new technologies and innovative ideas, driving sustained growth and success in a competitive landscape.

## 9.4 Tag Management in Healthcare and Life Sciences

Tag management within healthcare and life sciences is a critical aspect of data governance and operational efficiency. The deployment and administration of tags in this sector can significantly impact everything from patient record accuracy to regulatory compliance and operational workflows. The use of tags—in essence, identifiers assigned to various elements such as patient records, medical devices, and logistical items—enables enhanced tracking, categorization, and retrieval of information, ultimately leading to improved healthcare outcomes and streamlined processes.

One primary function of tag management in this environment is the enhancement of patient data management. Hospitals and clinics generate vast quantities of data every day, and the accurate tagging of patient records ensures that all relevant information about a patient's health history, treatments, and outcomes is readily accessible. This plays a crucial role in clinical decision-making, allowing healthcare providers to quickly retrieve comprehensive patient records, avoid potential errors, and deliver personalized care. Effective tag management ensures that all data is consistently and accurately tagged, reducing the risk of misidentification or data loss.

Additionally, medical research institutions benefit from sophisticated tag management systems. Research data is often voluminous and complex, necessitating rigorous organization for effective analysis and interpretation. Tags can be applied to categorize data by variables such as study type, methodology, patient demographics, and outcomes, facilitating more efficient data mining and pattern recognition. This capability is particularly invaluable in fields like genomics, where large datasets are common. Well-managed tags enable researchers to connect disparate data points, potentially leading to groundbreaking discoveries and innovations.

Regulatory compliance is another area where tag management is indispensable. The healthcare and life sciences sectors are heavily regulated, with stringent requirements for data handling and patient privacy, such as those stipulated by the Health Insurance Portability and Accountability Act (HIPAA) in the United States or the General Data Protection Regulation (GDPR) in the European Union. Tags help in maintaining compliance by ensuring that sensitive data is appropriately classified and access is controlled according to regulatory requirements. This can simplify audits and reduce the risk of non-compliance penalties.

In logistics and inventory management within healthcare settings, tag management also plays a fundamental role. Medical supplies, pharmaceuticals, and equipment need precise tracking to prevent shortages, overstocking, and ensure the timely and correct distribution. Radio-frequency identification (RFID) tags or barcodes are often employed to track the location and status of items across the supply chain. By using these tags, hospitals and pharmaceutical companies can maintain accurate records of inventory levels, monitor expiration dates, and even automate reordering processes, enhancing both efficiency and patient safety.

Operational efficiency within healthcare facilities further benefits from effective tag management. Workflow optimization is critical in environments where time-sensitive decisions and actions are routine. By tagging assets such as medical equipment, IT resources, and room availability, healthcare administrators can optimize their use and maintenance schedules. For example, in an emergency room setting, knowing the real-time status and location of critical medical devices can drastically reduce response times and improve patient outcomes.

Moreover, the integration of tag management systems with other healthcare IT solutions such as Electronic Health Records (EHRs), Laboratory Information Management Systems (LIMS), and Enterprise Resource Planning (ERP) systems can extend their utility even further. This integration provides a seamless flow of tagged information across various platforms, ensuring that all relevant data is consolidated and easily accessible for decision-making processes.

Finally, the advent of advanced technologies such as artificial intelligence (AI) and the Internet of Things (IoT) offers new horizons for tag management in healthcare and life sciences. AI can automate the tagging process, enhancing both speed and accuracy, while IoT devices equipped with tags can provide real-time data, enabling proactive management of healthcare operations. As these technologies evolve, the role of tag management will only grow more integral to the delivery of exceptional healthcare and the advancement of medical research.

In conclusion, tag management in healthcare and life sciences is essential for maintaining data integrity, ensuring regulatory compliance, optimizing logistics, and enhancing operational efficiency. Through the strategic assignment and management of tags, healthcare providers and researchers can unlock significant improvements in their workflows and outcomes, ultimately contributing to better patient care and pioneering advancements in medical science.

# 10. Market Dynamics and Tag Management

Navigating the intricate landscape of digital marketing requires a nuanced understanding of both the forces that drive market dynamics and the tools that facilitate effective campaign management. As businesses increasingly pivot toward data-driven strategies, the role of tag management systems (TMS) has become pivotal in capturing, analyzing, and leveraging customer data. This chapter delves into the confluence of market dynamics and tag management, offering a detailed exploration of how these elements interact to shape marketing success. By dissecting the mechanisms that influence market behavior and examining the operational efficiencies brought about by advanced tag management solutions, readers will gain a comprehensive framework for optimizing their marketing efforts in a rapidly evolving digital ecosystem.

## 10.1 Understanding Market Forces and Their Impact on Tags

Market forces play a crucial role in shaping the landscape of various industries, including those that deal with tags. Tags, in this context, encompass a broad spectrum—ranging from product tags, RFID tags, to digital tags used in online marketing. Understanding these market forces and their impact on the tag industry requires a deep exploration of several key elements: supply and demand, competition, technological advancement, regulation, and consumer behavior.

First and foremost, supply and demand are fundamental economic principles that influence the tag industry. A surge in demand for products often translates into a greater need for tags. For example, the e-commerce boom has significantly expanded the market for digital tags used in online tracking and product identification. Supply chains must adjust to meet this growing demand, which can influence the price and availability of raw materials used to produce tags. Additionally, shortages of certain materials, such as semiconductors for RFID tags, can disrupt supply chains and impact delivery timelines and costs.

Competition within the tagging industry also plays a pivotal role in shaping market dynamics. Companies continually strive to innovate and offer superior tagging solutions, which can range from more efficient RFID technologies to creative and cost-effective QR code designs. Competitive pressures drive the industry forward, compelling enterprises to invest in research and development, which can result in cutting-edge, more cost-effective, and efficient tagging solutions. This also means that smaller players might struggle to keep pace with larger, resource-filled competitors, potentially leading to market consolidation.

Technological advancement is another compelling force impacting the tag industry. Innovations in technology can lead to the development of smarter, more efficient, and versatile tags. For instance, advancements in RFID technology have led to tags that can store more data and be read at greater distances. Similarly, the evolution of Near Field Communication (NFC) technologies has enabled the creation of tags that facilitate contactless payments and information exchange. Technological progress, therefore, elevates the functionality of tags, making them more integral to various applications, from logistics to consumer electronics.

Regulation is a significant external market force that can shape the tag industry. Regulatory bodies across different regions impose guidelines and standards that manufacturers and users of tags must adhere to. For example, regulations concerning data privacy have considerable implications for digital and RFID tags used in tracking and data collection. These regulations ensure that sensitive consumer data is handled with utmost care and transparency. Companies must adapt to these regulatory requirements, which can involve modifying existing technologies or investing in compliant alternatives

Consumer behavior and trends are also instrumental in dictating the direction of the market for tags. As consumers grow more tech-savvy, their expectations for product information and interaction evolve. This has led to an increased demand for tags that can deliver rich, interactive experiences. For example, QR codes that lead to augmented reality experiences or product RFID tags that provide detailed production origin data resonate well with modern consumers. A shift towards sustainability is also influencing tagging solutions, with eco-friendly tags gaining popularity as consumers become more environmentally conscious.

In addition to these primary market forces, globalization and trade policies can have far-reaching effects. The global nature of supply chains means that economic or political shifts in one region can impact tag production and distribution worldwide. For example, tariffs or trade restrictions on components essential for manufacturing tags can lead to increased costs and delays.

Understanding market forces and their impact on the tag industry is a multifaceted endeavor that encompasses economic principles, competitive dynamics, technological innovation, regulatory frameworks, and evolving consumer behavior. Each of these forces interplays complexly to shape the current state and future trajectory of the tagging market. For stakeholders within this industry, whether they are manufacturers, distributors, or end-users, staying informed about these forces is crucial to making strategic decisions that align with market realities and capitalize on emerging opportunities.

## 10.2 Adapting Tag Strategies to Market Changes

In a rapidly evolving market landscape, the ability to adapt tag strategies is crucial for maintaining visibility and relevance. Tag strategies, encompassing the selection and usage of keywords, metadata, and other tagging methods, play a pivotal role in digital marketing, SEO, and content management. As market dynamics shift, these strategies must be flexibly adjusted to align with new trends, consumer behaviors, and competitive movements.

To begin with, understanding market changes involves ongoing research and analysis. This includes tracking keyword performance metrics, staying updated with industry reports, and utilizing tools like Google Trends, SEMrush, and Ahrefs that provide insights into shifting search queries and keyword popularity. Analytics platforms can help in identifying variations in organic traffic patterns, user engagement, and conversion rates, which can signal changes in consumer interests or market conditions. By closely monitoring these metrics, businesses can anticipate when their current tag strategies may need adjustments to better capture audience attention and maintain search engine rankings.

Adapting tag strategies often begins with keyword optimization. As search behaviors evolve, certain keywords may decline in relevance while new terms surface. Regularly updating keyword lists to reflect the latest trends ensures that content continues to resonate with target audiences. Long-tail keywords, which are more specific and less competitive, can also become more important as niche markets develop. By incorporating these into tag strategies, marketers can tap into highly targeted audiences with specific needs, thereby improving conversion potentials.

Metadata optimization is another critical component. Title tags and meta descriptions are not only influential in user click-through rates but also significant to search engine algorithms. These elements should be revisited regularly to ensure they align with current market language and trends. Crafting compelling, updated metadata that incorporates trending keywords can significantly boost organic traffic. Furthermore, utilizing schema markup to enrich metadata can provide search engines with better context about the content and improve its chances of appearing in rich snippets, thereby increasing visibility.

The dynamics of user-generated content and social media activity must also be integrated into tag strategies. As social platforms continuously introduce new features and algorithms, the way content is discovered and shared can change significantly. For instance, the rise of Instagram's algorithm favoring posts with certain hashtags or the increasing importance of Pinterest's keyword recommendations requires an agile approach. Keeping an eye on social media analytics can reveal emerging keyword trends specific to these platforms, enabling more effective tagging and categorization strategies that align with audience behaviors

Competitive analysis is an ongoing necessity when adapting tag strategies. Understanding the keywords and tags competitors are using can offer valuable insights. Tools like Moz's Competitive Analysis suite can help track competitors' keyword strategies. Observing shifts in their tagging techniques, such as the adoption of new keywords or changes in metadata, can offer clues about market shifts and potential opportunities for your own content strategies.

Another aspect is localization and personalization. As global markets become more interconnected and localized content grows in importance, businesses must adapt tags to cater to diverse regional audiences. This includes translating and localizing keywords and metadata to reflect local language nuances and cultural preferences. Personalization, driven by data analytics and AI, allows for the customization of content tags based on individual user behavior. Implementing adaptive tag strategies that adjust in real-time to user interactions can improve user engagement and retention rates.

In conclusion, adapting tag strategies is an iterative process that requires constant vigilance and responsiveness to market changes. By staying informed through diligent research, optimizing keywords and metadata, leveraging social media insights, analyzing competitive movements, and embracing localization and personalization, businesses can craft flexible, dynamic tag strategies. These strategies not only enhance visibility and relevance in a fluctuating market but also drive sustained growth and engagement, ensuring that content effectively reaches and resonates with evolving target audiences.

## 10.3 The Role of Tags in Responding to Competition

Tags play a crucial role in responding to competition within various fields, particularly in digital marketing, search engine optimization (SEO), content management, and social media strategies. They serve as pivotal tools that can help businesses and individuals enhance their visibility, improve user experience, and differentiate themselves from the competition.

In the realm of SEO, tags such as title tags, meta tags, header tags, and keyword tags are integral to improving a website's ranking on search engines. Title tags, for instance, are one of the most significant on-page SEO elements. They serve as the first impression users get of your website on search engine results pages (SERPs). Optimizing title tags with relevant keywords can make a website more attractive to potential visitors, thereby driving higher organic traffic. Meta tags, specifically the meta description, provide search engines and users with a brief summary of a webpage's content. Properly crafted meta descriptions can lead to higher click-through rates (CTR) because they provide a compelling call to action or highlight a unique selling proposition.

Header tags (H1, H2, H3, etc.) also play a vital role in structuring content and emphasizing its importance. Header tags not only make content more readable but also help search engines understand the hierarchy of your content. By strategically using header tags infused with target keywords, businesses can improve their search visibility, making it easier to compete with other companies in their niche.

Keyword tags, although less pivotal today than in the past due to search engine algorithm changes, still play a role in content categorization and searchability. By identifying and utilizing the right keywords, businesses can align their content with user search intent. This alignment makes it more likely for their content to appear in search results for relevant queries, thus outperforming competitors who may not be as precise in their keyword strategies.

In social media, hashtags function similarly to SEO tags by categorizing content, improving visibility, and facilitating engagement. Hashtags enable users to find posts related to specific topics or trends easily. When businesses use trending hashtags or create unique branded hashtags, they can reach a broader audience and elevate their competitive stance on social platforms. Furthermore, hashtags allow brands to participate in relevant conversations and tap into existing communities, thereby increasing their reach and engagement.

Web content management systems (CMS) such as WordPress leverage tags to streamline user navigation and improve the overall user experience. By tagging content effectively, website administrators can create an interconnected web of information that keeps users engaged and reduces bounce rates. Tags allow users to find related content easily, making the navigation experience seamless and intuitive. This user-centric design can differentiate a business from its competitors by fostering a more engaging, enjoyable, and informative experience for the audience.

Tags also play a role in e-commerce platforms where product tags can enhance product discoverability and categorization. For instance, tagging products with specific attributes, such as "organic," "handmade," or "eco-friendly," can attract niche markets and meet the needs of specific consumer preferences. Utilizing these tags effectively ensures that products reach the intended audience, thereby improving sales and customer satisfaction. Competing businesses that overlook the strategic implementation of product tags may miss out on these opportunities, giving attentive competitors an edge.

Furthermore, tags contribute significantly to analytics and performance tracking. By tagging marketing campaigns, content pieces, or social media posts, businesses can track which tags yield the highest engagement, conversions, or sales. This data-driven approach allows companies to refine their strategies and focus on areas that offer the best competitive advantage. In an environment where data and analytics drive decision-making, tags are indispensable tools for staying ahead of the curve.

In conclusion, tags serve multiple functions that are essential for responding to competition. Whether it's for enhancing SEO, improving social media engagement, optimizing web content navigation, categorizing products, or tracking performance, tags enable businesses to strategically position themselves in a competitive landscape. By leveraging tags effectively, companies can boost their visibility, appeal to target audiences, and make data-informed decisions that help them stay ahead of their competitors.

# 10.4 Case Studies of Market-Driven Tag Strategies

Market-driven tag strategies are essential tools for companies seeking to optimize their inventory and improve their understanding of customer preferences. By leveraging insights derived from real-world applications, businesses can create more responsive and adaptive supply chains. This section explores several case studies that highlight the efficacy of these strategies in various sectors.

## Case Study 1: Retail Fashion Sector

A high-end fashion retailer utilized market-driven tag strategies to track inventory in real-time. They implemented RFID tags on each clothing item, which provided them with immediate visibility into stock levels and customer preferences. As a result, they were able to reduce out-of-stock scenarios and quickly adapt to trends. For instance, a sudden spike in demand for a particular style allowed them to reorder and restock before losing potential sales. Consequently, customer satisfaction increased, and sales boosted by 20% within six months.

## Case Study 2: Grocery Store Chain

A large grocery store chain incorporated QR codes on its product tags to enhance customer engagement and streamline inventory management. These QR codes provided customers with detailed product information and allowed them to make informed purchasing decisions. Additionally, the data collected from these tags enabled the store to keep track of buying patterns, seasonal trends, and overall demand. The grocery chain effectively minimized waste by aligning its inventory with consumer preferences, leading to a 15% reduction in perishable goods waste.

## Case Study 3: E-commerce Business

An online retailer embedded advanced tag technology into its supply chain to better handle the complexities of digital marketplaces. Using beacon technology and NFC tags, the company could track shipping logistics and warehouse operations more accurately. Customers received real-time updates about their order status, increasing transparency and trust. Tag data also helped optimize warehouse layouts, proving instrumental in decreasing the time required to process and ship orders by 30%, thus enhancing customer experience and loyalty.

## Case Study 4: Electronics Manufacturer

A leading electronics manufacturer employed market-driven tag strategies to manage their extensive and varied product lineup. By leveraging IoT-enabled tags, each product could communicate with the company's central database, providing status updates on performance and usage. The collected data proved invaluable for R&D, as it highlighted common issues and areas needing improvement. This feedback loop ultimately fostered innovation and customer-centric product development and reduced return rates by 10%.

**Case Study 5: Health and Wellness Retailer**

A health and wellness chain used customer-driven tagging strategies that involved loyalty cards linked to individual purchases. By analyzing purchase data, the retailer could provide personalized recommendations and targeted promotions. Customers received discounts on frequently purchased items or products complementary to their buying habits. This personalization not only improved customer satisfaction but also drove a 25% increase in repeat customers over the year.

**Case Study 6: Automotive Industry**

An automobile manufacturer utilized market-driven tag strategies to enhance its production and after-sales services. RFID tags were attached to each vehicle part, offering detailed insights into the assembly line's efficiency and part utilization rates. In post-sales, these tags allowed dealerships to provide better maintenance schedules and recall processes. This end-to-end visibility streamlined manufacturing and service processes, leading to a 15% reduction in production costs and improved customer service quality.

**Case Study 7: Home Improvement Retailer**

A home improvement retailer implemented market-driven tag strategies for their vast and diverse product inventory. Using smart shelf tags updated in real time, the retailer ensured that stock levels and prices were always accurate. Tags also provided interactive content, such as product comparisons and DIY tips, enhancing the in-store experience. This innovation led to an 18% increase in average transaction values and a significant uptick in customer satisfaction.

**Case Study 8: Pharmaceutical Industry**

A pharmaceutical company used serialization tags to combat counterfeit drugs and enhance supply chain transparency. Each drug item received a unique serial number, trackable from manufacturing to patient delivery. This capability assured quality and authenticity to consumers and improved regulatory compliance. The outcome was a 40% decrease in counterfeit cases and higher consumer trust in the brand.

**Case Study 9: Logistics Company**

A global logistics company integrated RFID and GPS tags within its fleet to track cargo movement and condition. This tagging system provided real-time data on location, temperature, and humidity, crucial for sensitive shipments. It allowed for immediate corrective actions if deviations were detected. The integration improved punctuality and reduced spoilage rates by 22%, reinforcing the firm's reputation for reliable delivery.

**Case Study 10: Beverage Manufacturer**

A major beverage producer applied market-driven tagging to monitor production output and sales performance across different regions. Smart tags on each batch communicated data about production timing, ingredient sourcing, and shelf life. Sales data integration provided real-time analysis of regional preferences and seasonal demands. This information allowed the company to adjust production schedules and distribution plans proactively, reducing market mismatches and boosting sales by 17%.

In conclusion, these case studies illustrate the transformative impact of market-driven tag strategies across various industries. By enhancing inventory accuracy, customer satisfaction, and overall efficiency, these strategies have proven essential for businesses to stay competitive in a rapidly evolving marketplace.

# 11. Structuring Tag Management Teams for Success

Effective tag management is critical for ensuring streamlined data collection, robust digital analytics, and operational efficiency in today's fast-paced digital landscape. As organizations navigate the complex ecosystem of digital marketing and analytics tools, the success of their tag management efforts often hinges on the structure and capabilities of the teams responsible for it. This chapter delves into the strategic blueprint required to build and sustain a proficient tag management team.

Understanding how to structure such a team involves more than simply appointing skilled individuals. It requires a nuanced approach to defining roles, fostering collaboration, and implementing best practices that align with an organization's unique objectives and resources. We will explore the key components that constitute a high-performing tag management team, including the essential skills, roles, and responsibilities. Additionally, we'll examine the importance of cross-departmental synergy and the impact of leadership in driving team success.

By the end of this chapter, readers will gain comprehensive insights into the fundamental aspects that contribute to effective tag management team structures, enabling them to cultivate an environment where efficiency, accuracy, and innovation thrive. Whether you are building a team from scratch or looking to enhance an existing one, the strategies delineated herein will serve as a valuable guide to achieving excellence in tag management.

# 11.1 Organizing Teams for Effective Tag Management

Effective tag management is a crucial aspect of digital marketing and web analytics, ensuring that data collection, reporting, and overall website performance are optimized. For tag management to be successful, it requires not only the right tools but also the seamless collaboration of multidisciplinary teams. The organization of these teams directly impacts the efficiency and effectiveness of tag management.

To start, it's vital to clearly delineate team roles and responsibilities. This typically begins with identifying a tag management lead or a project manager who will oversee the entire tag management process. The tag management lead coordinates various tasks, manages timelines, and ensures that all team members are aligned with the project goals. This role is essential for maintaining order and ensuring that all tagging activities are executed smoothly.

Next, we have the analytics team, which plays a pivotal role in tag management. The analytics professionals are responsible for defining the requirements for data collection, ensuring that the right metrics are being tracked, and configuring tags to capture these metrics accurately. This team typically includes data analysts, measurement strategists, and data scientists. Their expertise is crucial in setting the foundation for successful tag management, as they understand the intricacies of data needs and can translate business objectives into measurable parameters.

The development team also plays a significant role in tag management. Developers are responsible for implementing and maintaining tag management solutions on the website. This involves coding and making necessary adjustments to ensure that tags are correctly placed and function as expected. They collaborate closely with the tag management lead and the analytics team to ensure that technical implementations meet the requirements set forth by the analytics team. Developers need to be adept at using tag management systems (TMS) such as Google Tag Manager, Adobe Launch, or Tealium iQ.

Furthermore, the marketing team cannot be ignored when organizing teams for effective tag management. Marketers rely heavily on data to make informed decisions, and thus, their input is integral during the planning and implementation phases. They need to communicate their needs effectively to the analytics and development teams, ensuring that all marketing activities are tracked precisely. This collaboration enables marketers to run campaigns with confidence, knowing that the required data will be available.

In addition to these core teams, it is beneficial to include a quality assurance (QA) team. The QA team's primary responsibility is to test the implemented tags to ensure they are firing correctly and collecting accurate data. This involves creating testing scenarios, using debugging tools, and analyzing data layers. The QA team works closely with developers to identify and rectify any issues that arise during testing, ensuring the reliability and accuracy of the data collected by the tags.

Another crucial component is documentation and communication. Effective tag management requires meticulous documentation of all tagging implementations, changes, and updates. This documentation should be accessible to all team members and should include detailed information about tag configurations, parameters, and data flows. Regular communication among team members is also essential to keep everyone informed about the status of tag implementations, issues encountered, and any changes in requirements.

Lastly, training and continuous learning are imperative for maintaining effective tag management practices. Teams should stay updated with the latest developments in tag management technologies and best practices. Regular training sessions, workshops, and knowledge-sharing meetings can help team members enhance their skills and stay proficient in their roles.

In summary, organizing teams for effective tag management involves a well-coordinated effort among various stakeholders, including tag management leads, analytics professionals, developers, marketers, and QA specialists. Clear roles and responsibilities, robust communication, thorough documentation, and ongoing training are the cornerstones of a successful tag management strategy. Each team member's contribution is vital for ensuring that tags are implemented correctly, data is accurately collected, and ultimately, that business goals are met through insightful analytics and data-driven decision-making.

## 11.2 Centralization vs. Decentralization in Tag Management

In the realm of digital marketing and web analytics, tag management systems (TMS) have become indispensable tools for managing and deploying marketing tags on websites. Within this domain, an ongoing debate persists: the merits and drawbacks of centralization versus decentralization in tag management. These two approaches represent fundamentally different strategies for handling the deployment, governance, and oversight of tags, and each has its unique advantages and challenges.

Centralization in tag management involves consolidating control and decision-making authority within a single team or department. Typically, this might be the IT department, a dedicated analytics team, or another specialized group responsible for managing and deploying tags. The primary benefit of this approach lies in its potential for consistent and standardized tag implementations. Centralized control helps ensure that all tags align with corporate policies, legal requirements, and technical standards, minimizing errors and reducing the risk of non-compliance. By concentrating expertise in one area, organizations can also benefit from deep domain knowledge and technical proficiency, leading to optimized tag performance and more efficient troubleshooting.

Additionally, centralized tag management can facilitate better data governance. With a focused team controlling all aspects of tag deployment, it becomes easier to enforce strict data collection protocols, maintain data quality, and ensure that users' sensitive information is handled appropriately. Security measures can be more robustly implemented, reducing the risk of unauthorized access or data breaches. Furthermore, having a central point of oversight allows for streamlined auditing processes, ensuring compliance with various regulatory frameworks, such as GDPR, CCPA, and other data protection laws.

However, centralization is not without its drawbacks. The most notable challenge is the potential bottleneck effect. When a single team is responsible for all tag management tasks, any delay or backlog within that team can slow down the deployment of new tags or the updating of existing ones. This can be particularly problematic in fast-paced environments where marketing teams need to respond quickly to emerging trends and opportunities. Additionally, centralization may lead to resource constraints, as the centralized team may be overly burdened with requests from multiple departments, each with its unique tagging needs.

In contrast, decentralization in tag management involves distributing the responsibility for tag deployment across several teams or departments. This approach empowers individual departments, such as marketing, sales, or product teams, to manage their own tags. One of the primary benefits of decentralization is increased agility. By allowing different teams to manage their tags independently, organizations can respond more swiftly to their specific needs and goals. This can lead to faster implementation of marketing campaigns, more timely updates, and greater overall flexibility.

Decentralization can also foster innovation. When individual teams have control over their tagging strategies, they can experiment more freely with new approaches, tools, and technologies. This autonomy can result in more creative solutions and greater experimentation, which may ultimately drive better performance and outcomes.

However, the decentralization approach presents significant challenges. The most pressing concern is the risk of inconsistency. Without a centralized framework, different teams may implement tags in ways that do not align with each other or with broader organizational goals. This can lead to fragmented data collection, difficulties in integrating data across systems, and potential compliance issues. Additionally, decentralized tag management may result in redundant or conflicting tags on the same web pages, slowing down page load times and negatively impacting user experience.

Another challenge is the potential for knowledge gaps. While decentralization allows for greater autonomy, it may also leave some teams without the necessary expertise to manage tags effectively. This can result in improper tag implementations, data inaccuracies, and suboptimal performance. Organizations adopting a decentralized approach must invest heavily in training and support to ensure that all teams have the skills and knowledge needed to manage their tags correctly.

Ultimately, the choice between centralization and decentralization in tag management depends on the specific needs and structure of an organization. Each approach offers distinct advantages and requires careful consideration of potential trade-offs. Many organizations find a hybrid approach to be the most effective, where centralized governance and oversight are combined with decentralized execution and flexibility, allowing them to reap the benefits of both strategies while mitigating their respective downsides. This balanced approach can facilitate better coordination, ensure data consistency, and drive more agile and innovative marketing practices.

## 11.3 Managing Cross-Functional Collaboration in Tag Deployment

Effective management of cross-functional collaboration in tag deployment is a critical component in today's data-driven business environment. The process of deploying tags involves inserting snippets of code into a website or application to collect and transmit data to various platforms for monitoring, analysis, and optimization purposes. In most organizations, several departments including marketing, IT, analytics, and product development, among others, need to work together to ensure that tags are deployed accurately and efficiently. This section delineates strategies for fostering and managing collaboration among these cross-functional teams to achieve seamless tag deployment.

First and foremost, setting up clear communication channels is fundamental. Given the technical complexity and varying priorities of each department involved, having a structured communication plan can significantly reduce misunderstandings and delays. Tools such as project management software, shared documentation platforms, and regular status meetings can facilitate transparency and keep everyone on the same page. Effective communication ensures that all teams are aware of the project timeline, component responsibilities, and any issues that arise, allowing for swift resolution and continuous alignment.

Another crucial aspect is defining roles and responsibilities. In many enterprises, ambiguity in role delineation can result in bottlenecks and overlapping duties, which in turn can hinder the tag deployment process. Creating a well-organized RACI (Responsible, Accountable, Consulted, and Informed) matrix allows team members to understand their specific roles and how they contribute to the broader objective. For example, the marketing team may be responsible for specifying the requirements of the tags, while the IT department handles the technical implementation, and the analytics team validates the data accuracy. Clearly defined roles can eliminate redundancy and ensure efficient task execution.

Furthermore, it is essential to implement standardized processes and best practices for tag management. This involves establishing a clear documentation process for all tag requests, deployments, and updates. Leveraging tag management systems (TMS) can provide a centralized dashboard for managing these tags, thereby streamlining workflows across various departments. With proper tagging protocols in place, organizations can minimize errors, ensure data integrity, and facilitate smoother tag audits and maintenance.

Training and knowledge sharing are also pivotal components of managing cross-functional collaboration. Each department should have a baseline understanding of the tag management process and the specific requirements that pertain to their roles. Conducting regular workshops, training sessions, and knowledge-sharing meetings can help bridge knowledge gaps and keep everyone updated on the latest tagging technologies and methodologies. A culture of continuous learning and mutual respect fosters an environment where team members feel empowered to contribute and collaborate effectively.

Risk management is another area that deserves attention. Tag deployment is often associated with various risks such as data privacy concerns, site performance issues, and potential disruptions to the user experience. Developing a comprehensive risk management plan involves identifying potential risks, assessing their impact, and devising mitigation strategies. For instance, implementing a testing phase before full-scale deployment can help identify and address any issues in a controlled environment, thereby ensuring a smoother rollout.

Lastly, measuring and reviewing the success of tag deployment initiatives is crucial. Establishing KPIs (Key Performance Indicators) for tag deployment projects can provide valuable insights into the effectiveness of cross-functional collaboration. Metrics such as deployment time, data accuracy, incidence of errors, and resolution times can help gauge performance and identify areas for improvement. Regularly reviewing these metrics and gathering feedback from all involved departments can drive continuous optimization of the collaboration process.

In summary, managing cross-functional collaboration in tag deployment requires a multifaceted approach involving clear communication, defined roles, standardized processes, continuous training, risk management, and performance measurement. By implementing these strategies, organizations can achieve more effective tag deployment, leading to improved data quality and enhanced decision-making capabilities.

## 11.4 Governance and Compliance in Tag Management Practices

In today's digital landscape, companies rely heavily on tag management systems (TMS) to streamline and optimize their digital marketing and analytics efforts. However, the convenience and power of TMS also bring forth significant governance and compliance challenges that must be meticulously managed. Effective governance and compliance in tag management practices necessitate a structured approach to ensure data integrity, privacy, and alignment with regulatory requirements.

Governance in tag management refers to the comprehensive framework of policies, processes, and accountability structures that govern the deployment and use of digital tags on a website. Good governance ensures that tags are implemented accurately, consistently, and in a way that aligns with organizational objectives. Effective governance starts with a clear policy that outlines the purpose and scope of tag management within the organization. Such policies should specify who is responsible for creating, reviewing, and updating tags, as well as who has the authority to approve and publish them.

One crucial aspect of governance is the establishment of a Tag Management Committee (TMC). The TMC should consist of cross-functional members from IT, marketing, analytics, legal, and compliance departments. This committee is responsible for overseeing the tag management process, making critical decisions about tag deployment, and ensuring that the practices are aligned with the company's strategic objectives and regulatory requirements. Regular meetings and a well-documented process for tag requests and approvals are vital to maintaining governance integrity.

The use of a tag audit process is another governance best practice. Regular audits help in identifying unauthorized tags, ensuring that existing tags are functioning correctly, and verifying that they are collecting and transmitting the intended data. Tag audits should be systematic and thorough, covering tag configuration, data payload verification, and data privacy compliance. Automated tag auditing tools can aid in this process by providing insights into tag performance and potential issues.

Compliance, on the other hand, focuses specifically on adhering to legal and regulatory requirements regarding data collection, processing, and storage. In the context of tag management, compliance ensures that tags do not violate user privacy or data protection regulations. Key regulations such as the General Data Protection Regulation (GDPR) in Europe and the California Consumer Privacy Act

(CCPA) in the United States place stringent requirements on how companies handle personal data.

To achieve compliance, companies must implement robust data protection mechanisms in their tag management practices. This includes tagging policies that enforce user consent before data collection, anonymization or pseudonymization of personal data, and ensuring data minimization principles are followed — collecting only the data that is necessary for the intended purpose. Additionally, companies must maintain transparent data usage policies and provide users with mechanisms to access, correct, or delete their personal data.

Another critical component of compliance is maintaining secure data transmission protocols. Tags often transmit data to third-party services for analytics and marketing purposes; therefore, it is essential that data transfer happens over secure channels (e.g., HTTPS) to protect it from interception or tampering. Furthermore, companies should perform regular security assessments of the TMS and any third-party vendors to ensure they meet security standards.

Documentation is a key element of both governance and compliance. Comprehensive documentation should include detailed information on all tags used, their purpose, data collected, consent management procedures, and any changes or updates to the tags. Proper documentation not only supports internal governance but also provides evidence of compliance with regulatory requirements.

In conclusion, governance and compliance in tag management practices are critical for maintaining data integrity, privacy, and adherence to regulations. By implementing structured policies, cross-functional committees, regular audits, robust data protection mechanisms, secure data transmission protocols, and comprehensive documentation, companies can effectively manage their tag ecosystems. This not only ensures compliance with legal requirements but also builds trust with users who are increasingly concerned about their digital privacy. Effective governance and compliance turn tag management from a technical necessity into a strategic asset, contributing to the overall success and credibility of the organization.

# 12. Sustainability and Tag Management

In the rapidly evolving digital landscape, businesses face an increasing need to manage their online presence efficiently while maintaining a focus on sustainability. As consumers grow more environmentally conscious, corporate strategies must integrate sustainable practices not only in production and logistics but also within the digital ecosystem.

This chapter delves into the intricate relationship between sustainable digital practices and effective tag management. By understanding the principles behind sustainability in the digital realm, we can explore how efficient tag management systems can contribute to a more eco-friendly online presence. From reducing data server loads to minimizing digital waste, the intersection of these two domains offers promising pathways for businesses to enhance their operational sustainability.

As we navigate through this discussion, we will examine case studies, best practices, and the latest innovations that illustrate the potential to harmonize digital efficiency with ecological mindfulness. This exploration aims to equip readers with the knowledge and tools necessary to implement sustainable tag management strategies, driving forward a commitment to environmental stewardship in the digital age.

# 12.1 Integrating Sustainability into Tag Strategies

The integration of sustainability into tag strategies necessitates a multifaceted approach. In the contemporary landscape, businesses, organizations, and even individuals are increasingly recognizing the importance of sustainability. Traditionally, tag strategies have been guided by factors such as market demands, competitive positioning, and technological advancements. However, the escalating urgency of environmental issues and the heightened awareness among consumers and stakeholders have introduced the imperative of incorporating sustainability considerations into tag strategies.

At its essence, sustainability refers to meeting the needs of the present without compromising the ability of future generations to meet their own needs. When applied to tag strategies, this principle involves the careful assessment and incorporation of environmental, social, and economic impacts. To effectively integrate sustainability, it becomes essential to establish a comprehensive framework that addresses these three pillars in a cohesive manner.

First, the environmental dimension encompasses resource management, waste reduction, and the mitigation of negative impacts on ecosystems. For instance, selecting materials that are renewable or have a lower environmental footprint for tags can significantly contribute to sustainability. This could involve using recycled materials, biodegradable substances, or implementing production processes that minimize emissions and energy consumption. Additionally, employing eco-friendly printing techniques and inks can further reduce harmful environmental effects.

The social dimension of sustainability is equally significant. This facet involves ensuring that the manufacturing processes for tags are equitable and do not exploit labor. Companies should scrutinize their supply chains to guarantee fair wages, safe working conditions, and non-discriminatory practices. By fostering ethical practices, businesses not only contribute to the well-being of workers but also build a positive brand image that resonates with socially-conscious consumers. Furthermore, engaging communities in the decision-making process related to tag production and usage can engender a sense of ownership and responsibility, thereby enhancing societal acceptance and support for sustainable practices.

Economic sustainability, the third pillar, focuses on long-term viability and profitability without sacrificing environmental and social responsibilities. This aspect underscores the importance of creating tag strategies that can withstand and adapt to market fluctuations, regulatory changes, and evolving consumer preferences. Adopting sustainable practices can also lead to cost savings in the long run, despite potential initial investments. For example, efficient resource utilization and waste management can reduce operational costs. Moreover, as consumers increasingly seek out sustainable products, businesses that proactively integrate these principles may gain a competitive advantage, driving higher sales and customer loyalty.

To successfully integrate sustainability into tag strategies, it is vital to employ a holistic approach that involves all stakeholders. An inclusive process might begin with a thorough stakeholder analysis to comprehend their expectations, values, and concerns. This step ensures that the developed strategies are not only viable but also aligned with stakeholder priorities. Collaboration with suppliers, customers, employees, and community members can facilitate the exchange of ideas and the co-creation of innovative solutions.

Measurement and transparency are also critical components of a successful integration process. Businesses should establish clear metrics for assessing the sustainability performance of their tag strategies. These metrics could include factors such as resource efficiency, carbon footprint, social equity indicators, and economic resilience. Regular reporting on these metrics not only facilitates continuous improvement but also enhances accountability and trust among stakeholders. Transparency involves openly communicating the goals, processes, and outcomes associated with sustainability initiatives, thus fostering a culture of integrity and responsibility.

Finally, the dynamic nature of sustainability necessitates ongoing education and adaptation. As new technologies and methodologies emerge, organizations should remain agile and willing to evolve their tag strategies to incorporate the latest advancements. Commitment to continuous learning and adaptation ensures that the strategies remain relevant and effective in addressing the ever-changing sustainability landscape.

In conclusion, integrating sustainability into tag strategies demands a comprehensive and inclusive approach. By addressing environmental, social, and economic dimensions in a balanced manner and engaging stakeholders in meaningful ways, businesses can not only reduce their negative impacts but also enhance their long-term resilience and competitive edge. Through transparency, measurement, and ongoing adaptation, organizations can foster sustainable practices that resonate with the values and expectations of modern consumers and stakeholders.

## 12.2 The Role of Ethical Tag Management in Building Trust

Ethical tag management plays a pivotal role in fostering trust between businesses and their stakeholders, especially in the current digital age where data privacy and security are paramount concerns. Tag management refers to the process of managing JavaScript and HTML tags that are used for tracking and analytics within digital applications. These tags can be very powerful in gathering data for improving user experience, targeted marketing, and overall business intelligence. However, with great power comes great responsibility. The ethical dimension of tag management involves ensuring data privacy, transparency, and user consent, which collectively help in building and sustaining trust.

Firstly, ethical tag management promotes transparency. Digital users today are more informed and cautious about the websites they visit and the applications they use. They demand transparency about what data is being collected, how it is being used, and who has access to it. Ethical tag management ensures that businesses provide clear and understandable information about their data collection practices. This means not only having an easily accessible privacy policy but also ensuring that this policy is written in plain language that users can understand. In doing so, businesses demonstrate respect for their users' right to know what is happening with their personal information, which is a fundamental aspect of building trust.

Secondly, ethical tag management emphasizes the importance of user consent. Before tags collect any data, users should be given the option to grant or deny permission. The General Data Protection Regulation (GDPR) in Europe and the California Consumer Privacy Act (CCPA) in the United States are legislations that have made it mandatory for businesses to obtain explicit consent from users before collecting their data. This consent must be informed, meaning users should know exactly what they are consenting to without being misled by vague or deceptive language. By obtaining clear and informed consent, businesses can build a foundation of trust as users feel more in control of their personal data.

Furthermore, ethical tag management should guarantee data security. Implementing robust security measures to protect the data collected via tags is crucial. This includes encryption, secure data storage, and regular audits to ensure compliance with data protection standards. By prioritizing data security, companies can protect themselves from data breaches that can severely damage trust and reputation. Ensuring data security signals to users that the company values their privacy and is committed to protecting their personal information from unauthorized access or misuse.

Another critical aspect is minimizing data collection to only what is necessary. Ethical tag management challenges companies to question what data they truly need and to avoid collecting superfluous or excessively granular data that could invade user privacy. This principle of data minimization is rooted in the ethical concept of reducing harm and respecting user privacy. By limiting data collection, companies reduce the risk of sensitive information being exposed and demonstrate a commitment to responsible data practices.

Lastly, accountability in tag management is essential. Businesses need to regularly review and audit their tag management practices to ensure they comply with ethical standards and regulatory requirements. This involves setting up internal policies and practices that enforce ethical data collection and usage, as well as being transparent with users about any changes to these practices. Being accountable also means having clear mechanisms in place for addressing user concerns or complaints regarding data privacy. Openness to scrutiny and willingness to make improvements based on feedback further solidifies a company's commitment to ethical practices and reinforces the trust placed in them by their users.

In conclusion, ethical tag management is indispensable for building trust in today's data-driven world. By ensuring transparency, securing user consent, prioritizing data security, minimizing data collection, and maintaining accountability, businesses can not only comply with legal mandates but also demonstrate a genuine commitment to respecting user privacy and earning their trust. This, in turn, fosters a more secure and trustworthy digital environment where users feel safe and valued.

## 12.3 Building Sustainable Tag Models

Creating sustainable tag models in the context of modern information systems requires a multifaceted approach that integrates technological, environmental, social, and economic considerations. As societies strive to balance the exponentially increasing demands for data with sustainable practices, it is essential to develop systems that are not only efficient but also resilient and adaptable to future needs.

At the core of sustainable tag models is the principle of efficient resource utilization. This begins with the selection of materials for the physical components of tagging devices, commonly known as RFID (Radio Frequency Identification) tags. Traditionally, these tags have been composed of plastics, metals, and silicon, which involve substantial environmental costs during production and disposal. Innovations in biodegradable and recyclable materials offer promising alternatives that minimize environmental impact. Utilizing organic polymers or even paper-based substrates can reduce the carbon footprint associated with manufacturing and disposal of tags.

In addition to materials, energy consumption is a critical factor in the sustainability of tag models. Passive RFID tags, which do not require a dedicated power source and are activated by the electromagnetic field from a reader, present a lower energy consumption model compared to active RFID tags that rely on internal batteries. However, the deployment of readers and the infrastructure to support high-frequency tag systems need to be optimized for energy efficiency. This can be achieved through low-power wide-area networks (LPWAN) and energy harvesting technologies that convert ambient energy from sources such as solar, kinetic, or radio frequencies into usable power for the tags and readers.

Interconnectivity and integration with existing systems are equally important in developing sustainable tag models. Seamless interoperability with other technologies such as IoT (Internet of Things) devices, blockchain for secure data tracking, and cloud-based databases ensures that tags can form part of larger, more efficient systems. This interconnectivity supports real-time data analytics, which can significantly improve supply chain management, inventory control, and waste reduction.

Sustainability also extends to the lifecycle of the tags; this includes not only their production and usage but also their decommissioning and disposal. Initiatives and regulations mandating the recycling or repurposing of RFID tags at the end of their life cycle are crucial. Furthermore, the development of software solutions that can manage the lifecycle of tags, predicting wear and encouraging maintenance or replacement before failure, can enhance the longevity and reliability of tagging systems.

From a social and economic perspective, building sustainable tag models must consider accessibility and equity. Tags should be affordable and feasible for small and medium-sized enterprises, not just large corporations, to adopt. This widespread adoption can be incentivized through subsidies, grants, or tax breaks aimed specifically at sustainable technologies. Additionally, fostering partnerships between private enterprises, government bodies, and non-profit organizations can help democratize access to advanced tagging technologies, ensuring that the benefits of improved efficiency and sustainability are widely shared.

Moreover, consumer transparency is integral to the sustainability of tag models. Clearly communicating the environmental benefits and lifecycle impacts of RFID tags to the end-users can drive consumer demand for sustainable practices. Labels indicating the use of eco-friendly materials or energy-efficient technologies in tags can influence purchasing decisions and encourage manufacturers to prioritize sustainability.

Developing cutting-edge software and algorithms to analyze the vast amounts of data generated by RFID systems takes on special importance. These analytical tools can offer insights into usage patterns, helping optimize tag deployment and minimizing unnecessary production. Machine learning and AI can predict and prevent inefficiencies in logistics and operations, which in turn reduces waste and conserves resources.

In conclusion, the journey to building sustainable tag models is not merely a technological challenge but a comprehensive endeavor that blends innovation in materials science, energy efficiency, lifecycle management, social equity, and economic feasibility. By embracing a holistic approach that prioritizes the planet and its people alongside profits, sustainable tag models can significantly contribute to the creation of smarter, more resilient, and environmentally friendly systems.

## 12.4 Challenges in Balancing Tag Management and Sustainability Goals

Organizations increasingly face the complex challenge of balancing tag management and sustainability goals within their digital landscape. In the modern era, where companies are under constant scrutiny from both consumers and regulatory bodies, efficiently handling these two crucial aspects is no trivial task. Tag management refers to the systematic approach to managing JavaScript and HTML tags used for tracking and analytics on websites. Sustainability goals, on the other hand, encompass a wide array of initiatives aimed at promoting environmental, social, and economic health.

One of the primary challenges lies in the fundamental objectives of each domain. Tag management systems (TMS) are primarily geared towards optimizing digital marketing efforts, personalizing user experiences, and garnering actionable insights through data collection. Sustainability goals, however, are centered around reducing the ecological footprint, ensuring ethical resource usage, and fostering long-term environmental stewardship. Balancing these objectives requires a nuanced understanding of both fields and a strategic approach to integrating them.

Another significant challenge is the technical complexity involved in aligning tag management with sustainability. Modern websites often rely on a multitude of third-party tags for various purposes such as analytics, marketing automation, customer support, and more. Each tag adds to the code base, increasing the overall size and load time of the web pages. This, in turn, can lead to higher energy consumption as servers need to process more data, and users' devices expend more power to render content. Reducing the number of tags or optimizing them can contribute to energy efficiency, aligning with sustainability objectives, but this must be done without compromising the quality of data and user experience.

Furthermore, the data privacy regulations such as GDPR and CCPA add another layer of complexity. These laws require organizations to obtain explicit consent from users before collecting their data through tags, enforce stringent data protection measures, and allow users the right to delete their data. Balancing these legal requirements with sustainability can be quite challenging. Overly aggressive data collection strategies can not only violate privacy regulations but may also be perceived as unsustainable practices due to the excessive use of resources for storing and processing data.

Additionally, effective tag management necessitates ongoing monitoring and frequent updates. Tags often need to be modified to ensure they capture the required data accurately and comply with any changes in regulations. On the sustainability front, organizations need to continuously evaluate their practices and implement more environmentally friendly measures. Coordinating these continuous improvement processes can strain internal resources, necessitating investments in specialized skills and tools.

Another dimension to consider is the financial implication. Implementing advanced tag management solutions and sustainability initiatives often involves significant upfront costs. Businesses, particularly small and medium enterprises, may find it hard to allocate budgets for both. Therefore, it becomes imperative to present a robust business case for the return on investment from these dual strategies. For instance, using a more efficient TMS can lead to reduced energy consumption and better data analytics, which might justify the initial expenditures both financially and environmentally.

Moreover, achieving a balance requires cultural shifts within organizations. Employees at all levels need to be educated and trained not only on the technical aspects of tag management but also on the importance of sustainability. Creating awareness and fostering a culture that values both efficient digital practices and environmental stewardship can drive the necessary behavioral changes.

Finally, partnerships and collaborations also play a crucial role. Collaborating with vendors who share similar sustainability values can help ensure that the third-party tags being used are optimized for energy efficiency. Additionally, engaging with industry groups, attending forums, and contributing to standards development can aid in adopting best practices that marry tag management with sustainability.

In conclusion, balancing tag management with sustainability goals is fraught with challenges ranging from technical complexities and regulatory compliance to financial constraints and cultural shifts. Addressing these challenges requires a multifaceted approach that leverages advanced tools, continuous education, strategic investments, and collaborative efforts. Businesses that can successfully navigate this balancing act stand to gain not just in terms of regulatory compliance and brand reputation but also in achieving long-term sustainable growth.

# 13. Tags and Social Impact

In an increasingly interconnected world, the way we categorize, share, and interact with information has undergone a profound transformation. One of the pivotal elements in this evolution is the use of tags—simple yet powerful markers that have reshaped how we navigate the digital landscape. From organizing personal archives to creating collaborative databases, tags facilitate a nuanced categorization that transcends traditional boundaries.

However, the significance of tags goes beyond mere organization. Their impact ripples through the fabric of our social interactions, influencing everything from online communities to cultural movements. In modern times, the deployment of tags has even sparked social revolutions and advocacy campaigns, highlighting their profound influence.

This chapter delves into the multifaceted role that tags play in our digital and social ecosystems. We will explore their origins, their technical underpinnings, and most importantly, their ramifications for social engagement and collective consciousness. Through case studies and analytical perspectives, we aim to uncover how these seemingly innocuous tools serve as catalysts for broader societal changes.

# 13.1 The Social Responsibility of Tag Management

The concept of social responsibility in the realm of tag management is an evolving and critical topic in the current landscape of digital marketing and data privacy. Tag management involves the process of managing JavaScript and HTML tags, which are primarily used for analytics and marketing optimization purposes on websites and mobile apps. As consumers become increasingly aware of data privacy issues, companies employing tag management systems (TMS) bear the significant responsibility of handling user data ethically and transparently.

Tag management systems simplify the deployment and governance of tags, which are small snippets of code embedded in digital platforms to gather information about user behavior, preferences, and interactions. These tags facilitate the collection of data for various purposes, including performance analytics, remarketing, personalization, and more. While these functions are pivotal for enhancing user experience and driving business growth, they also raise concerns around user privacy, data security, and corporate accountability.

Social responsibility in the context of tag management primarily entails ensuring that user data is collected and used in a manner that respects privacy and complies with pertinent regulations such as the General Data Protection Regulation (GDPR) and the California Consumer Privacy Act (CCPA). These regulations mandate that companies must obtain explicit consent from users before collecting their data, provide transparency regarding how the data will be used, and offer options to opt-out.

The ethical use of tag management systems begins with transparency. Companies must clearly communicate to users which data is being collected, for what purposes, and how it will be used. Privacy policies should be accessible, comprehensive, and comprehensible, avoiding technical jargon that can obscure the message. Transparency fosters trust between consumers and businesses and lays the groundwork for responsible data handling practices.

Another critical element is obtaining informed consent. Users should be empowered to make informed choices about their data. This means that consent mechanisms should be clear, concise, and designed to ensure that users truly understand what they are agreeing to. Popup notifications and consent banners should not be misleading or overly complicated. Moreover, companies should provide users with the ability to easily manage their consent preferences at any time, offering options to withdraw consent as effortlessly as it was given.

Data minimization is another fundamental principle that companies must adhere to. This principle dictates that only the data strictly necessary for the intended purpose should be collected and processed. Collecting excessive or irrelevant data not only exposes users to unnecessary risks but also breaches ethical guidelines and regulatory requirements. Implementing a robust TMS allows companies to streamline data collection processes, ensuring that tags are precisely configured to gather only the information that is essential and relevant.

Moreover, the implementation of proper data security measures is imperative. Companies must take all reasonable steps to protect the data they collect from breaches, unauthorized access, and misuse. This involves employing advanced encryption methods, regular security audits, and ensuring compliance with industry standards for data protection.

Employee training and awareness are also vital components of socially responsible tag management. Ensuring that employees understand the importance of data privacy and security, and are proficient in using the TMS correctly, is crucial. Regular training sessions and updates about current best practices and regulatory changes help maintain a high standard of data handling within the organization.

In addition to regulatory compliance and ethical practices, companies must also consider the broader implications of their data collection activities. This involves reflecting on how data-driven decisions might impact society at large, such as reinforcing biases or contributing to the digital divide. Responsible usage of TMS requires a commitment to using data in ways that promote fairness, inclusivity, and societal well-being.

For instance, while personalized marketing can enhance user experience, it should not encroach on user autonomy by manipulating or deceiving individuals. The ethical approach to leveraging data for personalization involves balancing business objectives with the respect for user autonomy and consent.

In conclusion, the social responsibility of tag management is an intricate aspect of modern digital operations that encompasses transparency, informed consent, data minimization, security, and ethical use. As digital footprints continue to grow, the onus is on companies to employ TMS in a manner that respects privacy, fosters trust, and contributes positively to the digital ecosystem. Responsible tag management is not only about compliance but also about building a sustainable relationship with consumers grounded in respect and trust.

# 13.2 Addressing Social Issues Through Tagging Initiatives

Tagging initiatives have emerged as a compelling means for addressing various social issues in contemporary society. This practice, which involves labeling or categorizing objects, locations, and even digital content with informative markers, aims to facilitate navigation, enhance understanding, and foster engagement among diverse groups. The power of tagging lies in its ability to bring attention to undervalued, misunderstood, or marginalized aspects of society, thereby promoting awareness, empathy, and action towards social change.

One of the foremost areas where tagging initiatives have been notably impactful is in urban environments. Cities around the world face multifaceted social issues, including homelessness, food insecurity, and crime. Tagging initiatives, leveraging technology such as Geographic Information Systems (GIS), have enabled activists, non-profits, and governmental agencies to map these issues comprehensively. For instance, tagging homeless populations' locations allows service providers to coordinate their efforts more effectively, ensuring that resources such as shelters, medical aid, and food distribution are optimally deployed. This tailored approach helps in bridging gaps between services and beneficiaries, ultimately aiming to reduce urban inequality.

A significant aspect of tagging in the digital realm involves social media platforms where hashtags play a crucial role. Tags such as BlackLivesMatter, MeToo, and ClimateStrike have created virtual communities rallied around pertinent social issues. These tags not only amplify individual voices but also drive collective action. They work as digital signposts that guide users to relevant content, discussions, and movements. For instance, the MeToo movement tagged millions of testimonies worldwide, which not only highlighted the prevalence of sexual harassment but also pressured institutions to adopt stringent policies against such behavior. The viral nature of these tags facilitates a global discourse, transcending geographical boundaries and acting as catalysts for legislative, cultural, and systemic changes.

Furthermore, tagging initiatives have made significant strides in the education sector, predominantly through digital tagging of educational content. Students from marginalized communities often lack access to quality education due to systemic barriers. Tagging initiatives have revolutionized access to information by making educational resources more searchable and accessible. Educational platforms that categorize content under tags such as STEMEducation, InclusiveEducation, and EnvironmentalScience enable students to easily locate materials that are otherwise obscure or out of reach in traditional academic settings. These tagged resources create an inclusive educational environment, empowering students with knowledge irrespective of their socio-economic background.

In the realm of environmental conservation, tagging initiatives are pivotal. Environmental activists and organizations use tagging to monitor and report on issues such as deforestation, wildlife trafficking, and pollution. Citizen science projects often rely on tagged data collected by volunteers, which is then used to track biodiversity and ecological changes. For instance, tags on species sightings contribute to databases that help scientists understand migration patterns, population dynamics, and threats to biodiversity. Such tagging not only raises public awareness but also drives community participation in environmental conservation, leading to more informed and engaged citizenship.

The importance of tagging initiatives becomes even more pronounced in the mental health domain. These initiatives are utilized to destigmatize mental health issues and create supportive communities. Tags like MentalHealthAwareness and EndTheStigma are used across various platforms to share personal stories, resources, and support networks. They facilitate access to critical information, such as symptoms, treatment options, and coping mechanisms. This virtual tagging fosters a sense of community and belonging, where individuals can seek help and share their experiences without fear of judgment. This communal support is crucial in an era where mental health issues are rising, acting as a bridge to professional help and societal acceptance.

In conclusion, tagging initiatives serve as powerful tools for addressing social issues by enhancing visibility, fostering community engagement, and facilitating the organization of information and resources. Whether through digital hashtags, GIS mapping, or educational resource categorization, tagging acts as a catalyst for social awareness, empathy, and action. By drawing attention to and organizing the myriad facets of social issues, tagging initiatives enable a more informed, connected, and proactive society.

# 13.3 Measuring the Social Impact of Tag Strategies

Understanding the social impact of tag strategies is pivotal in the current digital era, where the online presence of individuals, organizations, and communities significantly influences their reach and effectiveness. Tags, or metadata, help categorize content, making it easily searchable and thereby enhancing its discoverability on platforms such as social media, content management systems, and e-commerce websites. Measuring the social impact of these strategies involves a multi-faceted approach, combining quantitative and qualitative metrics to provide a comprehensive view of their effectiveness.

One of the fundamental aspects of measuring the social impact of tag strategies is through quantitative metrics. These metrics include engagement rates, reach, impressions, and click-through rates. Engagement rates pertain to the level of interaction that users have with tagged content, including likes, shares, comments, retweets, and other forms of active participation. High engagement rates typically indicate that the tags used are resonating well with the audience, generating discussions and furthering the spread of the content.

Reach and impressions are also crucial metrics. Reach refers to the number of unique users who encounter the tagged content, while impressions denote the total number of times the content is displayed, regardless of user interaction. A comprehensive analysis of reach and impressions can illuminate the breadth of the audience that the tag strategy is engaging with. For instance, a high reach with low engagement might suggest that the tags are effective at attracting viewers but are not compelling enough to foster interaction.

Click-through rates (CTR) are particularly important in e-commerce and digital marketing realms. CTR measures the effectiveness of a tag by analyzing the percentage of users who click on a tagged link out of the total users who view the content. High CTRs indicate that the tags successfully attract users and drive traffic to specific web pages or products, underscoring the commercial viability of the tag strategy.

On the qualitative side, sentiment analysis provides deeper insights into the social impact of tag strategies. Sentiment analysis involves examining the tone and context of user interactions with tagged content to discern whether the feedback is positive, negative, or neutral. This analysis helps organizations understand the emotional resonance of their tags and adjust their strategies to better align with their audience's preferences and concerns.

Moreover, the social impact can be measured by the alignment of tag strategies with overarching social goals, such as raising awareness on crucial issues, promoting community engagement, or facilitating resource sharing. For example, a non-profit organization using tags to promote a campaign on climate action can measure the impact by tracking the growth in community involvement, the spread of educational content, and the mobilization of resources and volunteers.

Another key aspect of measuring social impact is network analysis, which studies the interactions and connections that form around tagged content. Network analysis can map out how information spreads through different demographics and communities, highlighting influential tags and identifying key actors who drive the dissemination of content. This helps organizations optimize their tag strategies to target influential nodes within networks, thereby maximizing their social outreach and effectiveness.

Additionally, long-term tracking and longitudinal studies can provide insights into the sustainability and evolving impact of tag strategies. By analyzing data over extended periods, organizations can discern trends, adaptability, and the enduring influence of specific tags. This long-term view can inform more resilient and adaptable strategies that evolve in response to changing social dynamics and user behaviors.

Finally, stakeholder feedback plays an integral part in measuring the social impact of tag strategies. Direct feedback from users, community leaders, and other stakeholders provides firsthand insights into the effectiveness and reception of tag strategies. Surveys, focus groups, and interviews can uncover nuanced perspectives that are not readily apparent through quantitative data alone, thereby enriching the evaluation process with contextual depth and human insight.

In conclusion, measuring the social impact of tag strategies requires a holistic approach that integrates both quantitative and qualitative metrics. By combining various analytical tools and methodologies, organizations can gain a nuanced understanding of their tag strategies' effectiveness, enabling them to refine their approaches and maximize their social impact.

## 13.4 Case Studies in Socially Responsible Tag Management

Case studies have long been an important method to examine and understand the complexities of various systems and strategies in real-world situations. In the context of socially responsible tag management, they serve as invaluable tools to both dissect and demonstrate the potential benefits and challenges associated with implementing ethical practices in digital marketing and data collection.

Tag management refers to the process of managing the lifecycle of tags, or snippets of code, which are often used on websites to track visitor behavior, gather analytics, or implement third-party services such as advertising or social media integrations. Given the increasing concerns surrounding data privacy and security, socially responsible tag management has gained prominence. This practice emphasizes ethical considerations and compliance with data protection regulations.

One compelling case study involves a major e-commerce retailer that undertook a comprehensive overhaul of its tag management system to align with the General Data Protection Regulation (GDPR). Recognizing the sweeping implications of GDPR, which mandates robust protection of personal data for individuals within the European Union, the retailer invested in a GDPR-compliant tag management solution. This move was not only aimed at compliance but also at boosting consumer trust. The retailer ensured that all third-party tags were vetted for privacy implications, removed any non-essential tags, and provided clear information to users about data collection practices. Consequently, the retailer reported an increase in customer trust and a reduction in data breach risks.

Another illustrative case study focuses on a global news organization that was keen to demonstrate corporate social responsibility through its online presence. The organization adopted a transparent tag management policy aligned with the principles of ethical journalism. They employed a tag management system that gave users granular control over which types of data were collected about them. Users had the option to opt-out of tracking categories such as advertising or performance analytics, fostering a sense of empowerment and respect for user privacy. This initiative enhanced the news organization's reputation for integrity and ethical behavior, which attracted more privacy-conscious readers and advertisers.

A third case study involves a multinational financial services company that endeavored to balance the need for detailed analytics with strict regulatory compliance. By implementing a socially responsible tag management strategy, the company sought to comply with regulations such as the California Consumer Privacy Act (CCPA). The strategy involved anonymizing data wherever possible and obtaining explicit consent for data collection. By using advanced tag management software, the company could ensure that sensitive financial data was protected and that customers were given clear choices regarding their personal information. This move not only protected the company from potential legal repercussions but also reinforced its commitment to ethical practices.

The role of third-party vendors and their impact on socially responsible tag management cannot be understated. Another case study highlights a tech company's proactive approach in vetting its third-party partners. The company conducted comprehensive audits to ensure that all vendors adhered to the same high standards of data privacy and security. They established clear contractual obligations to safeguard user data and periodically reviewed these partnerships for compliance. This strict oversight reduced the risk of data leaks and enhanced the overall integrity of the company's digital ecosystem.

Lastly, an educational institution's experience offers insight into the implementation of socially responsible tag management in academia. Faced with the challenge of protecting student and staff data, the university incorporated a tag management system that prioritized data minimization and transparency. They offered detailed explanations about the purpose of each tag and sought informed consent for their use. This not only safeguarded individual privacy but also aligned with the institution's ethical values and regulatory requirements.

In conclusion, these case studies exemplify the vital role that socially responsible tag management plays across different sectors. From enhancing customer trust to ensuring regulatory compliance, the careful and ethical management of tags is indispensable in today's data-driven landscape. These real-world examples demonstrate that prioritizing ethical considerations in tag management is not only feasible but also beneficial in building lasting relationships with users and safeguarding organizational reputation.

# 14. The Future of Tag Management

As we step into an era marked by rapid technological advancements and increasingly sophisticated digital ecosystems, the role of tag management in online operations has never been more pivotal. Once considered a niche component within marketing and analytics, tag management has evolved into an essential, multifaceted powerhouse that supports a wide range of business imperatives, from data governance to user experience. In this chapter, we will explore the emerging trends and innovations shaping the future landscape of tag management. We will delve into how these advancements are poised to revolutionize the way organizations collect, manage, and leverage data, ultimately driving more informed decisions and strategic growth. Through expert insights and real-world examples, we aim to provide a comprehensive understanding of what lies ahead, preparing you to navigate and thrive in this ever-evolving digital terrain.

# 14.1 Emerging Trends in Tagging Practices

As the digital landscape continues to evolve, tagging practices have become increasingly sophisticated, reflecting both technological advancements and shifts in user behavior. Initially, tagging served as a straightforward mechanism to categorize and locate content more efficiently. However, today's tagging practices encompass a broader range of applications, including data analytics, content personalization, and search engine optimization (SEO). This transformation is driven by emerging trends that reshape how tags are created, managed, and utilized.

One prominent trend is the integration of machine learning and artificial intelligence (AI) to automate the tagging process. Previously, tags were manually assigned, a method that was both time-consuming and prone to human error. Modern AI algorithms can analyze content—be it text, images, or videos—and generate tags that are contextually relevant. This automated approach not only enhances accuracy but also scales efficiently, managing vast amounts of data without the need for continuous human intervention. Tools like Natural Language Processing (NLP) have made it possible to understand the nuances of human language, making automated tagging more intuitive and sophisticated.

In parallel, the trend towards using metadata for advanced data analytics has gained momentum. Tags are not just organizational tools; they provide valuable data points that help analyze user behavior, content performance, and engagement metrics. For instance, content creators and marketers can track which tags are most frequently clicked or searched, allowing them to gauge the interests and preferences of their audience. This data is instrumental in refining content strategies, developing targeted marketing campaigns, and improving overall user experience.

Another significant trend is the increasing emphasis on semantic tagging. Traditional tagging systems often relied on simple keywords, which had limitations in capturing the full context and meaning of the content. Semantic tagging, on the other hand, aims to understand and represent the relationships between different pieces of information. By embedding contextual meaning into tags, this method enhances the precision of information retrieval and makes content more discoverable. Semantic tags can link related concepts and entities, allowing for more nuanced and richer content interactions.

User-generated tagging, or folksonomy, is also experiencing a resurgence, albeit in a more structured form. While initially popularized by social media and web 2.0 platforms, user-generated tags suffered from inconsistencies and redundancy. Modern platforms are leveraging community input but are implementing checks to maintain quality and relevance. For example, algorithms can suggest tags based on popular usage while filtering out noise, thereby balancing the benefits of crowd-sourced insights with the need for order and coherence.

Moreover, tagging practices are becoming more pivotal in content personalization. Personalized experiences are increasingly in demand, and tags play a crucial role in tailoring content to meet individual preferences. Algorithms analyze user interactions with different tags to build detailed profiles that inform content recommendations. This has far-reaching implications across various domains, from e-commerce to entertainment, where delivering the right content to the right user at the right time is paramount.

Another emerging trend is the standardization of tagging practices across platforms and industries. With the proliferation of digital content spanning multiple channels, there is a growing need for a unified approach to tagging. Standardized tagging practices ensure interoperability and ease data integration across different systems. Organizations are increasingly adopting industry-specific tagging frameworks and best practices to streamline operations and maintain consistency.

Environmental sustainability isn't exempt from the impacts of tagging trends. Many companies are adopting eco-friendly content management systems, leveraging efficient tagging to reduce data storage requirements and energy consumption. Tags that facilitate data deduplication and optimized information retrieval contribute to a smaller digital footprint, aligning with broader sustainability goals.

In conclusion, emerging trends in tagging practices are reshaping the digital content landscape, enhancing how information is categorized, retrieved, and utilized. The integration of AI and machine learning, advancements in semantic tagging, and the resurgence of structured user-generated tags are collectively driving these changes. As tagging becomes more sophisticated and integral to digital ecosystems, it will continue to play a crucial role in optimizing content management, personalization, and data analytics, laying the groundwork for future innovations in the field.

## 14.2 Globalization and Its Impact on Tag Management

The phenomenon of globalization has significantly shaped various aspects of the digital landscape, including the specialized niche of tag management. Tag management refers to the process of managing tracking tags—snippets of code inserted into a website's HTML or JavaScript to collect data—using a centralized system or platform. These tags are vital for web analytics, advertising, customer relationship management (CRM), and a myriad of other digital strategies. With globalization accelerating at an unprecedented rate, its multifaceted impacts on tag management are profound and warrant thorough exploration.

First and foremost, globalization has facilitated the proliferation of international businesses and the expansion of companies beyond their domestic markets. This expansion necessitates more complex tag management systems capable of handling diverse data practices across multiple regions. For instance, multinational corporations may have different privacy laws and data protection regulations to navigate. The European Union's General Data Protection Regulation (GDPR), California Consumer Privacy Act (CCPA), and Brazil's General Data Protection Law (LGPD) are examples of legislation influencing how data is collected and managed. A modern tag management system must be adaptable to these regulations to ensure compliance and avoid hefty fines.

Further complexifying the landscape, globalization means dealing with an increasingly broad audience base that speaks various languages and exhibits different browsing behaviors. To effectively capture and analyze data for these diverse demographics, businesses must deploy tailored tags across multiple localized versions of their websites and applications. Advanced tag management solutions offer features like multi-language support and geo-targeting capabilities, making it easier for enterprises to maximize the relevancy and efficacy of their data collection efforts.

In addition to language and regulatory challenges, globalization intensifies the need for real-time data processing. As businesses grow globally, their digital footprint expands, leading to higher volumes of data traffic. Tag management systems must operate efficiently at scale, providing instantaneous data reporting and analytics to support timely decision-making. This real-time capability is crucial for optimizing digital marketing campaigns and improving user experiences on a global scale.

Moreover, the impacts of globalization stretch into the realm of cybersecurity. As companies expand and operate in multiple territories, they face a broader array of cyber threats. The global nature of these threats requires robust tag management systems that integrate effectively with cybersecurity frameworks to protect against data breaches and unauthorized data access. Some sophisticated tag management platforms offer features like tag auditing and real-time monitoring to ensure that security remains streamlined and foolproof.

Additionally, globalization fosters greater collaboration and innovation across borders, leading to advancements in tag management technologies. For example, cloud-based tag management solutions have emerged to meet the demands of a globally distributed workforce. These solutions offer the flexibility and scalability needed to manage tags across multiple geographic regions seamlessly. Collaborative tools and integrated platforms empower remote teams to align strategies and maintain consistency, regardless of location.

One of the salient benefits of globalized tag management is the ability to harness big data for comprehensive, multi-dimensional insights. By pooling data from different geographic regions, companies can perform more refined analytics, uncovering trends and patterns that would otherwise be overlooked. These insights feed into strategic decision-making processes, enabling businesses to tailor their offerings more precisely to meet the diverse needs of their international customer base.

Furthermore, the global nature of modern tag management introduces new opportunities for innovation in digital marketing. Increased connectivity enables the sharing of best practices and emerging trends across continents. This form of cross-pollination helps in the development of more sophisticated tagging strategies, enhancing the overall effectiveness of marketing campaigns. Companies can tap into a broader knowledge base, leveraging global expertise to fine-tune their tag management approaches for optimum performance.

In conclusion, globalization profoundly impacts tag management in several ways, ranging from regulatory compliance and data localization to cybersecurity and real-time data processing. It demands that organizations adopt highly adaptable and forward-looking tag management solutions to thrive in the global market. By doing so, businesses can improve accuracy, enhance user experiences, and secure a competitive edge in an increasingly interconnected world. As globalization continues to evolve, it is essential for businesses to stay abreast of its implications on tag management to navigate its complexities successfully while leveraging its vast opportunities.

# 14.3 Navigating Economic Uncertainty with Tag Insights

Economic uncertainty can present numerous challenges for businesses, governments, and individuals alike. Navigating the complexities of volatile markets, unpredictable fiscal policies, and unforeseen global events requires robust tools and strategies. One such emerging tool is Tag Insights.**Tag Insights** utilize data annotation methods to categorize and analyze large swathes of economic data, providing stakeholders with clearer perspectives and more actionable intelligence.

Tag Insights are predicated on the concept of tagging—assigning labels to discrete pieces of information, which can range from economic indicators like GDP growth rates to more qualitative data such as consumer sentiment expressed in social media posts. These tags help in systematically organizing information, making it easier to extract relevant patterns, trends, and correlations.

In practice, implementing Tag Insights begins with data collection from multiple sources. These sources could include traditional economic reports like those from the Bureau of Economic Analysis, market research data from private firms, and innovative streams like social media analytics and web scraping. This multipronged approach ensures a well-rounded view of the economic landscape.

Data tagging is both an art and a science. On one hand, it demands robust algorithms capable of identifying and categorizing data with precision. On the other hand, it requires human oversight to ensure that the tags are relevant and meaningful. Machine learning algorithms and natural language processing play a critical role at this stage. They automate the initial tagging process, identifying keywords, semantic structures, and other attributes that categorize each piece of information. Human analysts then review these tags for accuracy and relevance, refining the machine-generated tags as necessary.

Once tagged, the data can be fed into analytic models that offer deep insights into economic conditions. For example, by tagging news articles and social media posts with sentiments—positive, negative, or neutral—businesses can gain a real-time understanding of consumer confidence. This instant feedback mechanism can be invaluable for adjusting business strategies, such as modifying marketing campaigns or tweaking product offerings to align with consumer mood.

Governments can also benefit significantly from Tag Insights. Economic policymakers often need to make swift decisions based on incomplete data. The tagged datasets offer a quicker, more granular understanding of economic metrics, enabling more timely and effective policy interventions. For instance, during periods of rising inflation, tagged data can pinpoint specific sectors or regions experiencing the most pain, allowing for targeted fiscal measures rather than a broad-based approach.

Investors, too, stand to gain from this technology. Traditionally, investors rely on a slower cycle of quarterly financial reports and annual summaries to gauge the health of their investments. With Tag Insights, they can monitor real-time data that may signal market shifts before they become apparent in traditional reports. This proactive approach can provide a substantial edge in decision-making, allowing investors to either capitalize on emerging opportunities or mitigate impending risks.

It is important to note that despite its potency, Tag Insights is not infallible. Data quality remains a cornerstone of its effectiveness. Inaccurate tags or biased data inputs can lead to skewed analytics, which may result in suboptimal or even detrimental decisions. Therefore, a regular audit of both the tagging algorithms and the data sources is crucial to ensure ongoing accuracy and reliability.

Moreover, ethical considerations also come into play. The vast amount of data being tagged often includes sensitive information. Ensuring that this data is handled responsibly, with appropriate privacy measures and ethical guidelines, is paramount. Companies deploying Tag Insights must adhere to stringent data protection regulations like GDPR and CCPA to maintain consumer trust and avoid legal ramifications.

In conclusion, Tag Insights offer a promising avenue for navigating economic uncertainty. By leveraging advanced technologies to tag and analyze diverse datasets, businesses, governments, and investors can gain a deeper, more nuanced understanding of economic conditions. This, in turn, enables more informed decision-making, potentially reducing the adverse impacts of economic volatility. While challenges like data quality and ethical concerns must be diligently managed, the benefits of adopting Tag Insights in an uncertain economic landscape are compelling.

# 14.4 Preparing for the Future of Tag Management

Tag management, once a relatively straightforward aspect of website analytics and advertising, has evolved into a complex and multifaceted process. It requires ongoing attention, adaptation, and foresight to remain effective. Preparing for the future of tag management involves not only staying current with the latest technologies and best practices but also anticipating forthcoming changes that may affect the landscape. Here's how organizations can effectively prepare for the future of tag management.

## 1. Embrace Automation and AI

The future of tag management will likely see increased reliance on automation and artificial intelligence (AI). Machine learning algorithms can analyze vast amounts of data far more quickly and accurately than humans. They can identify patterns and make predictions that are practically impossible for traditional methods. By adopting AI-driven solutions, businesses can streamline their tag management processes, reducing human error and increasing efficiency.

## 2. Invest in Training and Skills Development

As technologies evolve, so must the skills of those who manage them. It is crucial to invest in continuous education and professional development for your team. This can involve attending industry conferences, participating in webinars, and completing relevant certifications. By staying ahead of the curve, your team will be better prepared to handle new tools and techniques.

## 3. Focus on Data Privacy and Compliance

One of the most significant challenges in the future of tag management is ensuring compliance with ever-changing data privacy regulations. Laws such as the General Data Protection Regulation (GDPR) in Europe and the California Consumer Privacy Act (CCPA) in the United States have set strict guidelines for data collection and management. It is imperative to stay informed about these and other regulations, implementing necessary changes to ensure compliance. Failure to do so can result in hefty fines and damage to your reputation.

## 4. Enhance Collaboration Between Teams

Tag management should not be isolated within the IT or marketing department; it requires a collaborative effort across various teams. Marketing, customer service, IT, and legal departments all have roles to play in effective tag management. Enhancing communication and collaboration between these teams can lead to more efficient processes and better data integrity. Tools like integrated project management software can aid in this endeavor, providing a centralized platform for communication and task management.

## 5. Prioritize Tag Governance

As the number of tags on websites continues to grow, so does the need for robust tag governance. This includes establishing clear policies and procedures for tag implementation, monitoring, and maintenance. Proper tag governance helps prevent issues such as tag bloat, duplicate tags, and data discrepancies. It is also essential for maintaining site performance, as too many tags can slow down site loading times, negatively impacting user experience.

## 6. Monitor Technological Advancements

The realm of tag management is continually evolving, with new tools and technologies emerging regularly. Keeping up with these advancements is vital for staying competitive. Subscribing to industry publications, participating in online forums, and networking with other professionals can help you stay informed about the latest trends and innovations.

## 7. Implement a Scalable Solution

As your business grows, your tag management needs will likely become more complex. Implementing a scalable tag management solution ensures that your system can handle increased traffic and data without compromising performance. Scalability also means that you can easily integrate new tools and technologies as they become available, ensuring that your tag management processes remain cutting-edge.

## 8. Evaluate and Optimize Regularly

Tag management is not a set-it-and-forget-it task. Regularly evaluating the performance of your tags and identifying areas for optimization is crucial. This can involve conducting periodic audits to ensure that all tags are functioning correctly and contributing valuable data. Optimization might include removing unnecessary tags, updating outdated ones, or consolidating multiple tags into a more streamlined setup.

## 9. Foster a Culture of Continuous Improvement

The most successful organizations are those that foster a culture of continuous improvement. Encourage your team to seek out new ways to enhance tag management processes, whether through new technologies, better practices, or innovative strategies. By prioritizing continuous improvement, your organization can stay ahead of the curve and be better prepared for the future.

**Conclusion**

Preparing for the future of tag management involves a multifaceted approach that encompasses technology, skills development, data privacy, collaboration, governance, and continuous improvement. By embracing these strategies, organizations can ensure that their tag management processes remain efficient, compliant, and poised to take advantage of the latest advancements in the field. The key to success lies in staying proactive and adaptable, ready to navigate the ever-changing landscape of tag management.

# 15. Scaling Tag Management Practices for Success

Chapter 15 delves into the pivotal role of scaling tag management practices to foster sustainable success. As digital ecosystems expand and marketing strategies become increasingly data driven, the need for a robust and flexible tag management system grows exponentially. This chapter will explore the methodologies and best practices that enable organizations to manage their tagging infrastructure effectively, ensuring that it not only keeps pace with growth but also enhances operational efficiency and data accuracy.

We will start by examining the foundational principles of tag management, establishing a common understanding of its core components and functionalities. Next, we'll discuss the challenges that come with scaling these practices, such as data overload, fragmented systems, and evolving regulatory landscapes. From there, we'll provide a comprehensive guide on developing a scalable tag management strategy, including insights on tool selection, cross-functional collaboration, and continuous optimization.

The insights shared in this chapter are crafted to equip you with the knowledge and tools required to elevate your tag management approach, ensuring that it remains agile, accurate, and aligned with your broader business objectives. Whether you are a seasoned marketing professional or just beginning to navigate the complexities of digital analytics, these strategies will help you build a resilient framework capable of adapting to ever-changing demands and accelerating your journey towards digital mastery.

# 15.1 Strategies for Scaling Tags Across the Organization

The effective implementation of tagging strategies across an organization can profoundly impact the management, retrieval, and utilization of information. Utilizing a systematic approach to scale tags can ensure consistency, enhance searchability, and support organizational goals. The following strategies are essential for successful tag scaling.

Firstly, developing a comprehensive taxonomy is foundational. A taxonomy is a structured classification that ensures tags are logical, hierarchical, and relevant to the organization's context. A well-devised taxonomy should be inclusive yet flexible, capable of evolving alongside the organization. The involvement of various stakeholders in the creation of this taxonomy is crucial as it ensures that diverse perspectives are considered, promoting a more universally applicable tagging system.

After establishing a taxonomy, the next step is to promote a culture of tagging within the organization. This involves training employees on the importance and application of the tagging system. Training sessions should be designed to cover not only the how-to but also the why behind tagging practices. Understanding the rationale encourages adherence and highlights the value of this process. Moreover, readily accessible documentation and continuous educational resources should be provided to support ongoing learning and adaptation.

Implementing a centralized tagging platform can streamline the process. A unified system that integrates with existing tools and workflows ensures that tags are consistently applied across various datasets and platforms. Centralized systems can also facilitate global updates and modifications, maintaining coherence throughout the organization. Such platforms often come with automated tagging suggestions based on machine learning algorithms, which can improve efficiency and accuracy.

Additionally, governance is vital to manage and sustain the tagging strategy over time. Establishing a governance framework involves defining roles and responsibilities for maintaining the taxonomy and tagging systems. A governance team should be tasked with overseeing the tagging process, resolving conflicts, and ensuring that the taxonomy evolves to meet the changing needs of the organization. Regular audits and evaluations can help in identifying and addressing inconsistencies, thereby maintaining system integrity.

Involving the end-users in the feedback loop is another critical strategy. Users who interact with the tagging system on a daily basis can provide insights into its functionality and areas for improvement. Creating channels for regular feedback and incorporating suggestions can refine the taxonomy and tagging practices, thereby enhancing their usability and relevance.

To further reinforce the tagging system, leverage analytics and reporting tools. By analyzing tagging metrics, such as frequency of tag usage and retrieval success rates, organizations can gauge the effectiveness of their tagging strategy. This data-driven approach allows for informed decisions regarding adjustments and improvements. Effective metrics and KPIs can also demonstrate the ROI of the tagging system to stakeholders, further legitimizing the program.

Incorporating automation can significantly enhance scalability. Automation tools can handle repetitive tagging tasks, reducing the manual effort required and human error potential. Technologies like Artificial Intelligence (AI) and Natural Language Processing (NLP) can automatically generate tags by parsing and understanding content. This not only increases the speed of tagging but also ensures a higher degree of consistency.

Ensuring data interoperability is another crucial aspect. Tags should be designed to work seamlessly across different systems and platforms within the organization. This requires a standardized set of metadata parameters that align with industry standards. Interoperability facilitates smoother data integration and exchange, ensuring that information tagged in one system can be effectively utilized in another.

Finally, fostering a collaborative environment is integral to the success of the tagging strategy. Encourage departments to share best practices and lessons learned from their tagging experiences. This cross-functional collaboration can lead to the discovery of innovative tagging solutions and the unification of disparate tagging practices. Regular meetings and forums for knowledge exchange can keep the momentum going and foster a community dedicated to optimal information management.

In conclusion, scaling tags across an organization requires a blend of strategic planning, technology integration, and cultural adaptation. With a robust taxonomy, comprehensive training, centralized platforms, effective governance, user feedback, analytics, automation, data interoperability, and cross-department collaboration, organizations can achieve a scalable tagging system that enhances information management and drives productivity.

## 15.2 Managing Tags in High-Growth Environments

Managing tags in high-growth environments requires a structured approach due to the inherent complexity and rapid pace of change. Tags, which serve as metadata associated with resources, people, or data, need careful management to ensure organizational efficiency and data integrity. This involves not only the technical aspects of creating and maintaining tags but also establishing robust governance frameworks to prevent chaos and confusion.

In high-growth environments, companies often experience rapid expansion in both scale and complexity. New products, services, resources, and employees are constantly added, which necessitates a scalable tagging strategy. One fundamental challenge is ensuring consistency in tag nomenclature, which is paramount for effective data retrieval and resource allocation. Without a standardized approach, different departments might develop their own tagging systems, resulting in fragmented and often redundant data sets.

A successful strategy begins with the establishment of a centralized tagging policy. This policy should define a standard vocabulary and tagging conventions that all employees must adhere to. For instance, a company might decide to use specific prefixes for tags associated with particular projects, departments, or regions. It is crucial to involve stakeholders from multiple departments when developing the tagging policy to understand their unique requirements and ensure buy-in.

Implementing automation tools can significantly enhance the efficiency of managing tags. These tools can be programmed to apply tags based on predefined rules, thus minimizing human error and the laborious task of manual tagging. Such systems can integrate with various platforms used by the organization, ensuring that tags are consistently applied across the board. For example, an AI-driven system can evaluate the content and context of a document and automatically assign appropriate tags.

To supplement automation, employee training is critical. Staff members must be educated on the importance of proper tagging and trained on how to use the tagging tools effectively. This training should be continuous to account for new employees and updates to the tagging system.

Regular audits of the tagging system can help identify and rectify inconsistencies. These audits involve reviewing a sample of tagged items to ensure adherence to the tagging policy. Discrepancies should be documented, and corrective actions should be taken to address any violations of the tagging standards. Additionally,

Cybellium - Google Tag Manager Certification

feedback gathered during these audits can be used to refine and improve the tagging system.

In high-growth environments, the sheer volume of data can be overwhelming. Therefore, it is essential to prioritize high-value tags that significantly impact business operations and decision-making processes. For instance, tags related to customer segmentation, regulatory compliance, and financial transactions might be given higher priority due to their critical nature.

Scalability is another crucial aspect. As the organization grows, the tagging system must be flexible enough to accommodate new categories and tags. This might require periodic revisions of the tagging policy to incorporate new business needs and technological advancements. Engage with technology partners or vendors to ensure that the tagging tools and systems remain up-to-date and capable of scaling with the organization's growth.

Secure management of tags is equally important. Tags often contain sensitive information, and improper handling can lead to data breaches. Therefore, access controls should be implemented to restrict who can create, modify, or delete tags. Logging and monitoring mechanisms can help track changes to tags, providing an audit trail that can be useful in compliance scenarios.

Furthermore, fostering a culture of accountability ensures that employees understand their role in maintaining the integrity of the tagging system. Regularly communicating the benefits of effective tag management, such as improved searchability, operational efficiency, and data-driven decision-making, can motivate compliance and diligence.

In conclusion, managing tags in high-growth environments demands a comprehensive approach that incorporates standardized policies, automation, employee training, regular auditing, and a focus on scalability and security. By addressing these elements, organizations can effectively manage their tags, leading to enhanced data integrity and operational success.

## 15.3 Expanding Tag Capabilities Globally

The expansion of tag capabilities on a global scale entails a comprehensive and multifaceted approach, driven by the increasing need for consistent and adaptable tagging systems across various industries and regions. Tags—small pieces of metadata attached to different forms of data—play a vital role in organizing, categorizing, and managing information in the digital landscape. The globalization of these capabilities is not only beneficial but necessary for the seamless integration of data management processes worldwide.

One fundamental reason for expanding tag capabilities globally is the escalating volume of data being generated every day. This data explosion, fueled by advancements in technology and the proliferation of digital platforms, requires sophisticated tagging systems that can keep up with diverse and ever-growing datasets. Expanding these capabilities ensures that data can be efficiently indexed, retrieved, and analyzed, regardless of its origin or format. As businesses and organizations increasingly operate on a global scale, uniform tagging practices facilitate better communication, decision-making, and strategic planning across borders.

Moreover, expanding tag capabilities on a global level promotes standardization and interoperability. Different regions and industries often develop their own tagging systems tailored to specific needs and contexts, leading to potential fragmentation and incompatibility issues. By establishing global standards for tagging, organizations can ensure that tags are universally understood and applied, enhancing the consistency and reliability of data usage. This effort requires collaboration among international regulatory bodies, industry associations, and technology developers to create and maintain comprehensive tagging frameworks that cater to a wide range of applications.

Another crucial aspect of global tag capability expansion is the incorporation of multilingual support. As organizations operate in multiple linguistic zones, tagging systems must accommodate various languages to be truly effective. This requires developing advanced natural language processing (NLP) technologies that can understand and generate tags in multiple languages, enabling accurate categorization and retrieval of data irrespective of the user's native language. Multilingual tagging not only bridges communication gaps but also opens up new opportunities for businesses to reach broader audiences and markets.

Security and privacy considerations also play a significant role in global tag capability expansion. Different countries and regions have varying regulations and standards concerning data protection and privacy. Expanding tagging capabilities globally involves designing systems that comply with diverse legal requirements, ensuring that tags are managed in ways that protect individuals' privacy and sensitive information. Implementing robust encryption and authentication mechanisms, along with regular audits and compliance checks, helps organizations mitigate risks associated with data breaches and unauthorized access.

Technological advancements such as machine learning (ML) and artificial intelligence (AI) are pivotal in driving the global expansion of tag capabilities. These technologies can automate the tagging process, making it faster and more accurate. ML algorithms can analyze large datasets, identify patterns, and generate relevant tags without human intervention, significantly reducing the time and effort required for data management. AI-powered systems can also adapt and learn from new data, continuously improving tagging accuracy and relevance over time. By leveraging these technologies, organizations can handle vast amounts of data with greater efficiency and precision.

Furthermore, the global expansion of tag capabilities necessitates the development of scalable and adaptable tagging infrastructure. As the volume and diversity of data grow, tagging systems must be capable of scaling up to meet the increasing demands. This involves implementing distributed and cloud-based architectures that can handle large-scale data processing and storage. Cloud platforms provide the flexibility and scalability needed to support global tagging operations, allowing organizations to manage data seamlessly across different regions and environments.

In conclusion, expanding tag capabilities globally is essential to address the challenges posed by the rapid growth of data, the need for standardization, multilingual support, security, and technological advancements. By fostering international collaboration and leveraging cutting-edge technologies, organizations can develop robust, compliant, and efficient tagging systems that enhance data management on a global scale. This expansion not only improves operational efficiency but also unlocks new opportunities for innovation and growth in the digital era.

# 15.4 Innovative Approaches to Scaling Tag Management

In the rapidly evolving digital ecosystem, the practice of tag management has emerged as a vital component of robust data strategy. Tags, which are snippets of JavaScript or HTML code, play a critical role in data collection, marketing, and customer analytics. However, as organizations grow in complexity and size, the challenges associated with tag management escalate, necessitating innovative approaches to effectively scale these operations. Here, we explore several such approaches that facilitate scalable tag management.

One of the primary approaches involves the implementation of comprehensive tag management systems (TMS). Modern TMSs, such as Google Tag Manager, Adobe Launch, and Tealium iQ, offer centralized platforms where tags can be easily managed, configured, and updated. These systems streamline the process of adding and modifying tags without directly altering the website's code, effectively reducing the risk of errors and enabling faster deployment times. Additionally, TMSs often come equipped with features like version control and debugging tools, which are indispensable for maintaining the integrity and performance of tags as they scale.

Another innovative approach to scaling tag management is the adoption of server-side tagging. Unlike traditional client-side tagging, where tags run in the user's browser, server-side tagging shifts the execution of these tags to a server environment. This shift not only enhances page load speeds and overall site performance but also provides greater control over data security and privacy. Server-side tagging minimizes the risk of data leakage and ensures compliance with stringent data protection regulations like GDPR and CCPA. The ability to handle large volumes of data without compromising speed or security makes server-side tagging a pivotal technique for scaling tag management.

Integrating artificial intelligence (AI) and machine learning (ML) into tag management processes is another frontier where significant advancements are being realized. AI-driven tag management tools can automate tag deployment and management by predicting and recommending optimal tagging strategies based on historical data and behavioral patterns. Machine learning algorithms can also assist in error detection and correction by continuously monitoring tag performance and flagging anomalies, thus reducing the burden on human resources and increasing operational efficiency. As these technologies continue to mature, their role in scaling complex tag management operations will only become more pronounced.

The use of container tags represents an additional method for scaling tag management efficiently. Container tags act as a single repository for multiple tags, significantly simplifying the management process. By encapsulating several tags into one container, organizations can reduce the number of individual tag requests, which in turn enhances page load times and reduces the risk of tag-related issues. This approach also facilitates easier updates and maintenance, as changes can be made to the container tag instead of updating each individual tag separately.

Data governance and standardization practices are crucial for scaling tag management effectively. Establishing a clear framework for how tags should be implemented, monitored, and maintained ensures consistency and reduces the risk of discrepancies across different departments or regions. Organizations should develop tagging guidelines and enforce strict compliance to these standards to maintain data quality and accuracy, particularly as the scale of operations expands. Regular audits and continuous monitoring can help in identifying and rectifying any non-compliance issues promptly.

Furthermore, collaboration between IT and marketing departments is essential for scaling tag management successfully. The often siloed nature of these departments can lead to inefficiencies and miscommunication, particularly when dealing with large-scale and complex tagging requirements. By fostering a collaborative environment where both IT and marketing teams work together, organizations can ensure that tagging efforts are aligned with broader business objectives, thereby optimizing both technical and marketing outcomes.

Lastly, robust training and education programs for staff involved in tag management cannot be overlooked. As new technologies and methodologies emerge, it is imperative that personnel are well-versed in these innovations to fully leverage their potential. Continuous training programs help in keeping the team updated with the latest best practices, tools, and techniques, thereby enhancing overall efficiency and effectiveness in scaling tag management operations.

In conclusion, the necessity of innovative approaches to scaling tag management cannot be overstated in today's data-driven world. By leveraging modern TMSs, adopting server-side tagging, integrating AI and ML, utilizing container tags, enforcing data governance, fostering cross-departmental collaboration, and investing in continuous training, organizations can effectively manage and scale their tagging operations to meet the demands of a growing digital landscape.

# 16. Corporate Strategies in Tag Management

In today's rapidly evolving digital landscape, the strategic management of tags has become an essential component for corporations aiming to optimize their online presence and marketing efficacy. Tag management systems (TMS) offer businesses the agility to deploy and oversee various marketing tags without necessitating ongoing IT involvement, thereby enhancing operational efficiency and speed to market.

This chapter delves into the multifaceted approaches corporations employ to leverage tag management effectively. It presents a comprehensive examination of the best practices adopted by industry leaders, explores innovative solutions tailored to complex organizational needs, and elucidates the potential pitfalls and challenges encountered in the realm of tag management. By providing detailed case studies, strategic frameworks, and actionable insights, this chapter aims to equip business leaders, marketing professionals, and IT teams with the knowledge necessary to master the intricacies of tag management and achieve sustainable competitive advantage in their digital initiatives.

# 16.1 Strategic Partnerships and Their Impact on Tagging

Strategic partnerships have always played a crucial role in the business world by allowing companies to collaborate, share resources, and achieve common goals. Specifically, in the context of tagging—which involves the assignment of metadata to digital content—strategic partnerships can have a profound impact. Tagging is a fundamental aspect of data categorization, improving searchability, and enabling more sophisticated data analysis and personalization. In this section, we will explore the multifaceted benefits that strategic partnerships bring to the practice of tagging, their influence on technological advancements, and the specific use cases where partnerships have revolutionized tagging mechanisms.

One of the foremost benefits that strategic partnerships offer to tagging is the enhancement of technological capabilities. Companies specializing in various dimensions of data management, artificial intelligence (AI), and machine learning can bring their expertise together to develop more sophisticated tagging algorithms. For instance, a partnership between a cloud storage service provider and an AI firm can lead to the creation of more intelligent, context-aware tagging systems. These systems can not only automatically tag content based on predefined categories but also learn and adapt over time, providing more accurate and relevant tags.

Moreover, strategic alliances can facilitate the integration of tagging functionalities into broader digital ecosystems. For example, a content management system (CMS) might partner with a social media platform to allow seamless tagging across both systems. This integration can enable a more unified tagging strategy, ensuring that content is consistently categorized no matter where it is published. The resulting interconnected tagging system can create a more coherent user experience and streamline content management processes.

In addition to technological advancement and integration, strategic partnerships can also significantly impact the standardization of tagging practices. Different industries and sectors often face challenges regarding the consistency of tags, which can lead to inefficiencies in data retrieval and analysis. By forming partnerships, companies can work together to develop industry-wide tagging standards. These standardized tags can facilitate easier data sharing and better interoperability between different systems, thus maximizing the usability of the tagged data.

Specific use cases also demonstrate the transformative power of strategic partnerships on tagging. In the realm of e-commerce, for instance, partnerships between retailers and machine learning startups can lead to the deployment of advanced product tagging systems. These systems can automatically tag products with attributes such as color, size, style, and even predicted customer preferences, thus significantly enhancing the online shopping experience. Shoppers can more easily find products that match their criteria, and retailers can benefit from higher conversion rates and customer satisfaction.

Similarly, in the field of digital marketing, partnerships can lead to more effective content tagging strategies that improve targeting and personalization. A digital marketing firm might collaborate with a data analytics company to develop a tagging system that categorizes content based on user behavior and preferences. This partnership can enable more precise targeting of advertisements and personalized content delivery, thereby boosting engagement and ROI.

The impact of strategic partnerships on tagging is also evident in efforts to improve content accessibility. Companies focusing on accessibility can partner with those specializing in AI to create tagging systems that identify and label content in ways that make it more accessible to people with disabilities. For instance, an AI-powered tool can automatically generate alt text for images, ensuring that visually impaired users receive a descriptive tag that conveys the image's content. Such efforts can broaden the audience for digital content and promote inclusivity.

Furthermore, strategic partnerships can facilitate the expansion of tagging technologies into new and emerging markets. A partnership between an established tech company and a local firm in a developing market can help tailor tagging solutions to the specific needs and contexts of that market. This can ensure that the tagging technologies are culturally relevant and meet the linguistic and contextual nuances of the local user base.

In summary, strategic partnerships can profoundly influence the landscape of tagging by driving technological progress, enabling system integration, standardizing practices, and demonstrating effectiveness across various use cases. These collaborations harness the strengths of each partner, leading to more intelligent, efficient, and inclusive tagging systems that benefit both businesses and end-users. By leveraging strategic partnerships, companies can stay ahead in the ever-evolving digital world and maximize the value derived from their digital content.

## 16.2 Mergers, Acquisitions, and Their Impact on Tag Management

Mergers and acquisitions (M&A) represent significant events in corporate strategy often intended to enhance competitive advantage, expand into new markets, or acquire new technologies. However, they also pose considerable challenges, especially in the realm of digital marketing and analytics. One critical aspect that often undergoes dramatic changes during M&A activities is tag management.

Tag management refers to the process of managing JavaScript and HTML tags used on websites for tracking and analytics purposes. Tags are essential for collecting data on user behavior, conversions, and other marketing metrics. Effective tag management ensures that data from various tools such as Google Analytics, AdWords, and third-party marketing platforms is accurate and efficiently collected.

The impact of M&A activities on tag management can be profound and multifaceted. Firstly, the integration of disparate web properties often necessitates the consolidation of various tag management systems (TMS). Companies merging or acquiring others may initially have multiple TMS platforms in place, each configured differently depending on their legacy requirements. Unifying these into a single, standardized system becomes crucial for streamlined operations. This unification ensures that data collection processes are consistent, accurate, and aligned with organizational goals.

Secondly, discrepancies in data architecture require substantial attention. Different firms may employ different naming conventions, data layer structures, and tagging methodologies. Harmonizing these variations is essential to maintain the integrity of data analytics. For example, if one company tracks user actions using event-based tags while the other uses pageviews, a comprehensive strategy must be employed to reconcile these differences. A failure to correctly align these tagging frameworks can lead to inconsistencies, data loss, and ultimately, misguided decision-making based on faulty analytics.

Another critical impact area is compliance with legal and data privacy standards. M&A activities often expose organizations to different regulatory environments, especially if the merged entities operate in diverse geographic locations. For instance, the General Data Protection Regulation (GDPR) in Europe imposes stringent requirements on data collection and consent. Integrating tag management systems must, therefore, ensure that compliance protocols are uniformly enforced across all digital assets. This may involve revisiting cookie consent mechanisms, user data storage policies, and opt-out functionalities.

Operational efficiency is also a significant consideration. Duplication in tags and inconsistent tagging practices lead to increased page load times and degraded user experience. Efficient tag management during M&A requires auditing and cleaning up redundant tags while optimizing the remaining ones for performance. This streamlining process not only improves website speed but also ensures more reliable data collection since redundant or conflicting tags can distort analytical insights.

The human element in M&A cannot be overlooked. Technology and processes are only as effective as the people who manage them. Often, M&A activities result in personnel changes and shifts in responsibilities. It is crucial to ensure that staff involved in tag management are well-versed in the unified platform and methodologies being adopted. Comprehensive training programs and clear documentation are indispensable for smooth transitions. A lack of expertise or knowledge gaps can easily result in errors that compromise data quality.

Finally, a strategic perspective is necessary for future scalability. As organizations grow and evolve, their tag management needs will shift. An M&A scenario provides an opportunity to re-evaluate and future-proof the tag management strategy. This might include adopting more advanced tools that offer better scalability, flexibility, and integration capabilities. Forward-thinking approaches ensure that as new digital initiatives come into play, they can be seamlessly incorporated into the existing framework without extensive rework.

In summary, mergers and acquisitions exert significant impact on tag management through the need for system consolidation, data architecture harmonization, compliance alignment, operational efficiency improvements, workforce training, and strategic scalability planning. Handling these aspects proficiently ensures that the integrated enterprise can maintain robust data analytics capabilities, providing a solid foundation for informed decision-making and sustained competitive advantage.

## 16.3 Innovation in Corporate Tag Strategies

In the rapidly evolving landscape of corporate branding, innovation in tag strategies has emerged as an indispensable facet for companies striving to achieve and maintain competitive advantage. Corporate tag strategies, often abbreviated as taglines or slogans, encapsulate the essence of a company's brand identity in a brief, memorable phrase. The development and deployment of innovative tag strategies can significantly influence a company's public perception, customer engagement, and overall market position.

One prominent example of an innovative corporate tag strategy is the transition from purely descriptive slogans to more aspirational and emotionally resonant taglines. Historically, many companies opted for taglines that were straightforward descriptions of their products or services. However, as the market began to flood with more players and the differentiation based solely on product features became challenging, brands shifted towards creating emotional connections with their audiences. This shift marked the inception of taglines designed to inspire, motivate, or evoke trust and loyalty among consumers. For instance, Nike's "Just Do It" transcends its role in identifying athletic wear; it speaks to the broader human experience of overcoming challenges and pursuing goals.

Another pivotal shift in corporate tag strategies has been the integration of social and environmental consciousness. In the modern marketplace, consumers are increasingly aware of and concerned about corporate social responsibility (CSR). Thus, many companies incorporate aspects of sustainability, ethical practices, or community impact into their taglines. This not only helps in building a positive brand image but also aligns with the values of conscientious consumers. A case in point is Patagonia's tagline, "We're in business to save our home planet." This tagline not only communicates the company's commitment to environmental stewardship but also cultivates a sense of shared purpose with its customer base.

Technological advancements have also brought about significant innovations in tag strategies. The advent of digital marketing and social media has necessitated that taglines be versatile and adaptable across diverse media platforms. This has led to the creation of taglines that are not only succinct and impactful but also capable of facilitating engagement through various digital channels. For example, taglines that work well as hashtags can enhance a company's social media presence and participation. Coca-Cola's "Share a Coke" campaign leveraged a tagline that could double as a hashtag, encouraging consumers to post and share their personalized Coke bottles on social media, thereby creating a dynamic and interactive branding experience.

Moreover, the rise of data analytics and consumer insights has revolutionized the customization of corporate tag strategies. Companies now utilize big data to understand consumer preferences, behavior, and demographics to craft tailored taglines that resonate more effectively with their target audiences. This data-driven approach allows for the creation of taglines that are not only catchy but also intimately aligned with consumer identities and aspirations, thus increasing brand relevance and loyalty.

Another trend in innovative corporate tag strategies is the utilization of humor and wit. In an era where consumers are bombarded with advertisements and brand messages, a touch of humor can differentiate a brand from the mundane and make it more memorable. Geico's "15 minutes could save you 15% or more on car insurance" combines informational value with a quirky appeal, making it both informative and entertaining.

Lastly, the dynamism of the global market has encouraged companies to adopt multilingual and culturally nuanced taglines. As brands expand their reach to international markets, it becomes crucial to craft taglines that are not only translated accurately but also culturally resonant. This involves a deep understanding of local languages, idioms, and cultural contexts to ensure that the tagline conveys the intended message without losing its impact or risking misinterpretation.

In conclusion, innovation in corporate tag strategies is not merely about crafting clever phrases but about creating meaningful connections and differentiating the brand in a crowded marketplace. By embracing emotional resonance, social responsibility, technological adaptability, data-driven customization, humor, and cultural sensitivity, companies can develop compelling taglines that not only capture the essence of their brand identity but also foster enduring relationships with their audiences. As the business landscape continues to evolve, the importance and intricacy of innovative tag strategies will undoubtedly expand, reflecting the ever-changing dynamics of consumer engagement and brand leadership.

# 16.4 Corporate Governance in Tag Policy Implementation

Corporate governance refers to a set of systems, principles, and processes by which a company is directed and controlled. In the context of tag policy implementation, corporate governance plays a critical role in ensuring that technology is used ethically, efficiently, and in accordance with organizational goals and legal requirements. Tag policies, which often involve the implementation and management of metadata tags across digital assets, can hinge on sound governance to manage risks, ensure compliance, and maximize value.

Firstly, corporate governance in tag policy implementation requires a clear governance framework. This framework should encompass defined roles and responsibilities, stipulating who is responsible for creating, managing, and enforcing tag policies. Typically, this includes senior leadership, IT managers, data stewards, and compliance officers. Establishing a cross-functional governance team can help ensure that various perspectives are represented, and that policies are aligned with the strategic objectives of the organization.

This governance model must include well-documented policies and procedures that dictate how tags should be used. This may involve specifying criteria for tag creation, standardizing tag formats, and defining acceptable tag types and usage scenarios. Clear guidelines help prevent inconsistencies, reduce errors, and facilitate effective data management. Policies should also address issues such as data privacy, security, compliance with regulations like GDPR or HIPAA, and regular audits to ensure ongoing adherence.

A critical aspect of corporate governance in this realm is risk management. Risks associated with poor tag policy implementation can include legal ramifications, data breaches, and loss of public trust. To mitigate these risks, organizations must conduct comprehensive risk assessments to identify potential vulnerabilities. This typically includes data encryption strategies, access controls to restrict who can create or modify tags, and regular monitoring for unusual activity that may indicate a security threat.

Training and communication are equally important for the successful implementation of tag policies. Employees across all relevant departments should receive training on the importance of tag policies, how to apply them, and the consequences of non-compliance. This training should be ongoing to reflect changes in technology, regulations, or corporate strategy. Additionally, effective communication channels ensure that any issues, concerns, or suggestions related to tag policy can be promptly addressed by the governance team.

Furthermore, technology tools play a vital role in facilitating tag policy implementation under a robust governance framework. These might include metadata management software, automated tagging systems, and compliance monitoring tools. Investing in the right technology can help ensure that tags are consistently and accurately applied, reducing the likelihood of human error and enhancing data reliability.

In the realm of performance measurement, governance should establish clear metrics and KPIs to evaluate the effectiveness of tag policy implementation. This might involve tracking the accuracy of tags, compliance rates, the speed of data retrieval aided by proper tagging, and overall user satisfaction. Regular reviews and audits should be conducted to assess these metrics, identify areas for improvement, and make necessary adjustments to the governance framework or policies.

Effective corporate governance in tag policy implementation is also contingent on leadership and culture. Organizational leaders must champion adherence to tag policies and model best practices. This top-down approach fosters a culture of accountability and compliance, encouraging all employees to take tag policies seriously. Moreover, promoting a culture of continuous improvement encourages feedback and innovation, ensuring that tag policies evolve in response to emerging challenges and opportunities.

Lastly, feedback loops are essential for refining governance practices. Regular feedback from stakeholders, including end-users, IT staff, and compliance teams, provides valuable insights into the practical challenges and successes of tag policies. This feedback should be systematically collected and analyzed to inform policy updates, training programs, and strategic decisions.

In conclusion, corporate governance in tag policy implementation is comprehensive and multifaceted, requiring a blend of clear frameworks, risk management strategies, effective training, and the right technological tools. Through diligent governance, organizations can ensure that their tag policies uphold ethical standards, legal compliance, and contribute to organizational efficiency and strategic goals.

# 17. Metrics and Evaluation in Tag Management

In the rapidly evolving landscape of digital marketing, the implementation of effective tag management systems has become not just a convenience but a necessity. The ability to track, analyze, and optimize user interactions hinges on how well we deploy and manage these tags. However, the benefits of tag management are only fully realized when we establish clear metrics and a robust evaluation framework.

This chapter delves into the critical aspects of metrics and evaluation in the context of tag management. It seeks to equip you with the knowledge to measure the performance of your tags accurately, ensure data quality, and derive actionable insights. By understanding these metrics, you will be better positioned to refine your tagging strategies and maximize the impact of your digital marketing efforts. Through a combination of theoretical concepts and practical applications, this chapter aims to bridge the gap between tag management and data-driven decision-making, empowering you to make more informed, effective choices in your marketing initiatives.

# 17.1 Key Performance Indicators (KPIs) for Tag Success

In the ever-evolving world of digital marketing, tracking the success of your campaigns and initiatives is critical to ensuring your efforts are producing the desired outcomes. One essential tool for this purpose is Key Performance Indicators (KPIs). KPIs are measurable values that help organizations gauge how effectively they are achieving their key business objectives. When it comes to tag success – which refers to the tracking snippets (or tags) running on websites and applications to gather data about user interactions – having a solid set of KPIs is crucial. These KPIs provide insights into how well your tags are performing and whether they are driving the intended results.

To effectively measure and optimize tag performance, it is important to establish a well-rounded set of KPIs. Each KPI should align with specific goals and outcomes you aim to achieve with your tagging efforts. Here are several key KPIs that can provide a comprehensive understanding of your tag success:

**1. Tag Firing Rate:** This KPI measures the percentage of times a tag successfully fires when it is supposed to. If a tag has been configured to fire upon the completion of a form submission, for example, the tag firing rate would indicate how often this happens relative to the number of form submissions. A high tag firing rate suggests that your tags are working as intended, while a low rate may indicate issues with tag deployment or configuration.

**2. Data Accuracy:** Ensuring that the data collected through tags is accurate is paramount. Data accuracy can be measured by comparing the data captured by tags with data from other reliable sources. Any significant discrepancies may highlight issues such as tag misconfiguration, duplication, or firing errors.

**3. Load Time Impact:** Tags can affect the load time of your website. This KPI measures the impact of tags on the page load time. Optimizing tag load times is critical, as slow load times can adversely affect user experience and lead to higher bounce rates. Tools like Google Tag Manager provide insights into the performance overhead introduced by tags.

**4. Conversion Rate:** A critical aspect of tag success is its ability to track and measure conversions effectively. This KPI looks at the percentage of users who complete a desired action, such as making a purchase or signing up for a newsletter. By indicating how well your tags capture key conversion events, you can better understand the effectiveness of your marketing efforts.

**5. Error Rate:** This KPI tracks the frequency of errors associated with tags, such as failed tag fires or incorrect data transmission. A high error rate can compromise data integrity and reduce the reliability of your analytics. Monitoring and addressing tag errors promptly ensures that your data remains valid and actionable.

**6. Coverage:** Coverage measures the extent to which your tags are deployed across critical touchpoints on your website or application. Comprehensive coverage ensures that you are capturing relevant data from all crucial areas, providing a complete picture of user interactions and behavior.

**7. Tag Redundancy:** Excessive or redundant tags can clutter your site and potentially lead to performance issues. This KPI assesses the presence of unnecessary or duplicate tags that do not add value. Regular audits can help identify and eliminate redundant tags, thereby streamlining your tagging infrastructure.

**8. Event Tracking:** Event tracking is crucial for understanding user interactions beyond simple page views. This KPI measures the effectiveness of tags in capturing event data such as clicks, downloads, or video plays. Well-implemented event tracking tags provide deeper insights into user engagement patterns.

**9. Attribution Accuracy:** Accurate attribution is key to understanding which marketing channels and touchpoints drive conversions. This KPI evaluates how well your tags support multi-channel attribution models. Proper attribution allows for more informed budget allocation and campaign optimization.

**10. User Privacy Compliance:** With increasing regulations around data privacy, it's vital to ensure that your tags comply with legal requirements such as GDPR or CCPA. This KPI tracks compliance by auditing tags to ensure they respect user consent and privacy preferences. Non-compliance can risk legal repercussions and damage brand reputation.

**11. Scalability and Flexibility:** As your marketing initiatives evolve, so too should your tagging framework. This KPI assesses how scalable and flexible your tag implementation is to accommodate new requirements. A robust tagging system should be easily adjustable to incorporate new tags and adapt to changing business needs without sacrificing performance.

**12. Data Layer Utilization:** The data layer is a crucial component that enhances tag functionality by storing and managing data that tags can readily access. This KPI evaluates how effectively your tags use the data layer to store and transmit data, ensuring a structured and organized tagging approach.

**13. Cross-Device Consistency:** In a multi-device environment, ensuring consistent tagging across desktops, tablets, and mobile devices is essential. This KPI measures the uniformity of tag performance and data capture across various devices, ensuring a seamless user tracking experience.

**14. Tag Debugging Efficiency:** The efficiency with which issues related to tags are identified and resolved can significantly impact the overall success of your analytics efforts. This KPI tracks the average time taken to debug and fix tag-related issues, promoting a culture of rapid response and continuous improvement.

**15. Tag Update Frequency:** The digital landscape is constantly changing, and so should your tags. This KPI measures how frequently tags are reviewed and updated according to the latest standards and practices. Regular updates ensure that tags are aligned with current business goals and technological advancements.

**16. Vendor Tag Performance:** Many organizations use third-party vendor tags for additional functionality such as retargeting or A/B testing. This KPI assesses the performance and impact of these vendor tags, ensuring that they contribute positively to your overarching digital strategy.

**17. Tag Governance:** Effective governance policies are crucial for maintaining the integrity of your tagging infrastructure. This KPI evaluates the adherence to governance standards, including documentation, version control, and stakeholder accountability. Robust governance practices help maintain tag accuracy and reliability over time.

By diligently tracking and analyzing these KPIs, you can gain a clear and comprehensive understanding of your tag performance. Optimizing these indicators will not only enhance your data collection efforts but also improve the overall effectiveness of your digital marketing campaigns.

# 17.2 Measuring the Effectiveness of Tag Strategies

To effectively evaluate the impact of tag strategies, a systematic approach is critical. Tags, as a fundamental element in digital marketing, data organization, and content management, can significantly influence the visibility, accessibility, and user engagement of digital content. Leveraging the right metrics and methodologies to measure the effectiveness of these strategies offers invaluable insights for optimization.

**Defining Key Performance Indicators (KPIs)**

The first step in measuring the effectiveness of tag strategies involves defining clear and relevant Key Performance Indicators (KPIs). KPIs should align with the overarching goals of the digital content or marketing campaign. Common KPIs include website traffic, click-through rates (CTR), conversion rates, and user engagement metrics such as time spent on a page or the number of interactions per session. Additionally, metrics like search engine ranking, bounce rate, and social media shares can offer further insights into how tags are influencing content reach and quality.

**Data Collection and Analysis**

With KPIs established, the next phase is data collection. Utilizing web analytics tools like Google Analytics, Adobe Analytics, or specialized tagging platforms can facilitate this process. These tools can track a wide array of metrics, from user behavior to referral sources. Comprehensive data collection should encompass both quantitative metrics—such as the number of visits or clicks—as well as qualitative data, including user feedback and comments.

Once collected, data analysis involves identifying patterns and correlations. For example, one can analyze if specific tags are consistently associated with higher engagement rates. This analysis can help in pinpointing which tags drive more traffic or conversions. Tools with advanced analytical capabilities, such as machine learning algorithms, can detect non-obvious patterns and provide deeper insights.

**A/B Testing**

A/B testing—also known as split testing—is a proven method for gauging the effectiveness of different tag strategies. By creating two versions of a webpage, email, or other digital content—each incorporating a different set of tags—one can monitor and compare their performance. Critical metrics to compare include user engagement, conversion rates, and overall traffic. A/B testing allows for an iterative approach to optimization, where ineffective tags can be discarded in favor of those that demonstrate a clear performance boost.

## Heatmaps and User Interaction Metrics

Heatmaps are visual tools that represent user interactions on a webpage, showing areas where users click, scroll, or hover most frequently. Tools like Crazy Egg or Hotjar can generate heatmaps that help identify how effective certain tags are in attracting user attention. If a tag consistently appears in high-traffic areas as shown by heatmaps, it can be inferred that this tag contributes positively to user engagement. Conversely, tags associated with areas of low interaction may need reevaluation.

## SEO Performance

Search Engine Optimization (SEO) plays a pivotal role in digital content visibility, with tags such as meta titles, descriptions, and alt tags for images being integral to SEO strategy. Monitoring SEO performance metrics like organic search traffic, search engine rankings, and click-through rates from search results can provide insights into the effectiveness of these tags. Tools such as SEMrush, Ahrefs, or Moz offer functionalities to track these metrics and identify which tags are improving search performance.

## User Behavior Analysis

Evaluating user behavior is another critical aspect. By employing user behavior analytics, organizations can understand how tags influence the customer journey. Tools like Mixpanel or Amplitude track user actions and attribute them to specific tags, thus revealing how tags contribute to conversions or other desired actions. For instance, if a tag leads users to a call-to-action button that sees a high conversion rate, it can be deemed effective.

## Feedback Loop

Continuous improvement requires incorporating a feedback loop into the tag strategy measurement process. Regularly reviewing performance metrics, conducting user surveys, and staying updated with industry best practices help in refining tag strategies. Tools that offer real-time data and automated reporting can facilitate a proactive approach to tag management.

In conclusion, the effectiveness of tag strategies can be measured through a combination of well-defined KPIs, comprehensive data collection and analysis, A/B testing, heatmaps, SEO performance metrics, and user behavior analysis. Integrating a feedback loop ensures continuous optimization, ultimately driving better engagement, higher conversion rates, and improved overall performance. By systematically evaluating these aspects, organizations can maximize the impact of their tag strategies.

## 17.3 Benchmarking Tag Performance Across Industries

Benchmarking tag performance across industries is a crucial practice for businesses looking to optimize their tagging strategies and improve their overall digital marketing efficiency. This process involves analyzing and comparing the performance of different tags used in online advertising, website analytics, and other digital marketing tools across various sectors. By examining the effectiveness of these tags, businesses can gain valuable insights that help them refine their marketing strategies, enhance user experience, and maximize returns on investment.

Tags are small snippets of code or pixels embedded in webpages and digital ads, which track user behavior, measure campaign success, and gather valuable data. These tags play an essential role in digital marketing by providing information that helps marketers understand how users interact with their website or ads. The proper implementation and optimization of these tags are essential for achieving accurate analytics and improving marketing outcomes.

One fundamental aspect of benchmarking tag performance is setting clear objectives. Different industries may have varying goals and key performance indicators (KPIs) that define success. For instance, an e-commerce company might focus on conversion rates and average order value, while a media company may prioritize user engagement and session duration. By identifying specific metrics that align with industry objectives, businesses can ensure a more meaningful comparison and understand the context of their tag performance.

Data collection is another critical component of benchmarking tag performance. To gather accurate and comprehensive data, businesses must implement a robust tagging infrastructure. This typically involves using tag management systems (TMS) that facilitate the deployment and monitoring of tags without the need for extensive coding. Highly efficient tag management ensures that data is collected consistently across all relevant touchpoints, providing a reliable foundation for benchmarking activities.

Analyzing tag performance involves examining several metrics. These include tag loading times, data accuracy, and the impact on site performance. Fast-loading tags are essential for maintaining a positive user experience, as slow-loading tags can lead to increased page load times and potentially drive users away. Data accuracy is equally important, as discrepancies in collected data can lead to misguided decisions and strategies. Evaluating the impact of tags on site performance helps businesses balance the need for comprehensive data collection with the necessity of maintaining a smooth user experience.

One approach to benchmarking tag performance is to compare against industry standards and best practices. Many industry reports and studies provide valuable insights into common tag performance metrics within specific sectors. By utilizing these resources, businesses can gauge where they stand relative to their peers and identify areas for improvement. For example, a report might reveal that the average tag load time for the finance industry is significantly lower than that of the retail industry, prompting retailers to explore optimization opportunities.

Peer comparison is another beneficial strategy for benchmarking. Businesses can collaborate with industry partners or networks to share anonymized tag performance data. By doing so, they can gain a clearer understanding of how their performance stacks up against similar companies. This collaborative approach also fosters an environment of continuous learning and improvement, as businesses share insights and strategies for better tag management.

Technology and tool advancements play a crucial role in improving tag performance benchmarks. Emerging solutions, such as server-side tagging, offer enhanced efficiency and control over data collection. Server-side tagging processes data on the server rather than the client side, resulting in faster load times and improved data security. As businesses adopt these innovative tools, the overall standards for tag performance continue to evolve, setting new benchmarks for others to follow.

In summary, benchmarking tag performance across industries is a dynamic and multi-faceted process that requires a clear understanding of objectives, meticulous data collection, comprehensive analysis, and continuous collaboration. By embracing these practices, businesses can enhance their tagging strategies, optimize digital marketing efforts, and ultimately achieve superior results in the competitive digital landscape.

# 17.4 Auditing and Reviewing Tag Management Practices

Auditing and reviewing tag management practices are critical components in ensuring the efficiency, accuracy, and security of digital tagging systems within an organization. Tag management is the process of managing JavaScript and HTML tags used for tracking and data collection on websites. These tags facilitate various functionalities such as analytics, advertising, and user experience enhancement. For the successful deployment and performance of these tags, regular auditing and reviewing are essential.

The primary objective of auditing tag management practices is to verify that all tags are functioning correctly and that they comply with organizational policies and industry standards. This involves several steps. First, a comprehensive inventory of all tags currently deployed must be taken. This includes identifying the purpose of each tag, its locations, and the specific data it collects. A detailed inventory helps in maintaining an organized structure and ensures that no redundant or obsolete tags are present on the website.

One crucial aspect of the auditing process is assessing the performance impacts of tags. Tags can significantly affect the loading speed of web pages, which in turn can influence the user experience and search engine rankings. Auditors should use performance monitoring tools to measure the loading times of pages and identify any tags contributing to delays. Any tags that adversely affect site performance should be optimized or removed.

Security and privacy compliance is another critical area during the tag audit. Regulatory frameworks such as GDPR, CCPA, and other data protection regulations require that user data is collected and processed following strict guidelines. Auditors must ensure that all tags comply with these laws and do not collect unauthorized personal information. This often involves checking for proper consent mechanisms and verifying that data is transmitted securely.

After the initial audit, regular reviews should be instituted to keep the tag management practices up-to-date. The digital landscape is ever-evolving, with frequent updates to regulations, tools, and best practices. Continuous reviews help in adapting to these changes promptly. These reviews typically involve re-evaluating all tags to ensure they still serve a valid purpose and checking for updates or modifications needed for compliance and performance improvements.

Moreover, every tagging system should have a change management process. This process documents any changes made to the tagging system, including updates, additions, or removals of tags. Proper documentation and version control help in tracking changes over time, quickly identifying any issues arising from recent updates, and rolling back if necessary. This enhances accountability and minimizes risks associated with untracked changes.

Standardization plays a fundamental role in effective tag management. Organizations should develop and enforce tagging standards and guidelines that all team members must follow. These guidelines include naming conventions, data governance policies, and standard procedures for tag implementation and testing. Compliance with standardized practices ensures consistency, reduces errors, and simplifies future audits and reviews.

Automated tools can significantly aid in the auditing and review processes. Tag management systems like Google Tag Manager, Adobe Launch, and Tealium offer built-in functionalities for monitoring and auditing tags. These tools can automate inventory checks, performance monitoring, and security assessments, making the processes more efficient and less error-prone.

In conclusion, auditing and reviewing tag management practices are indispensable for maintaining effective, efficient, and compliant digital tagging systems. The processes involve comprehensive inventories, performance assessments, security and privacy compliance checks, regular reviews, change management, and standardization, all supported by automated tools. Properly conducted audits and continuous reviews not only ensure optimal performance and compliance but also enhance the overall digital strategy of an organization. Regular attention to these practices upholds the integrity and functionality of tag management systems, fostering a reliable and user-friendly online presence.

# 18. Barriers to Effective Tag Management

Tag management is a critical element in the orchestration of any sophisticated digital marketing strategy. It involves the meticulous organization and deployment of tracking codes, otherwise known as tags, which serve to measure and analyze a host of performance metrics across web properties. Despite its importance, effective tag management often encounters numerous barriers, posing significant challenges to marketing and IT teams alike.

In this chapter, we delve into the multifaceted obstacles that can impede the seamless execution of tag management. From technical constraints and data privacy concerns to organizational misalignment and resource limitations, these barriers are varied and complex. Understanding their nature and impact is essential for developing robust solutions that can ensure efficient and effective tagging practices.

We will explore common issues such as the integration difficulties between disparate systems, the evolving landscape of regulatory requirements, and the potential for performance degradation caused by poorly managed tags. Additionally, we will discuss the human factors at play, including the need for specialized skills and the importance of fostering interdepartmental collaboration.

By the end of this chapter, readers will gain a comprehensive insight into the root causes of these barriers and be equipped with practical strategies to overcome them. Addressing these challenges head-on is crucial for harnessing the full potential of tag management systems, ultimately driving more precise and actionable business insights.

# 18.1 Common Challenges in Managing Tags

In the realm of digital marketing and website management, the concept of tags refers to the snippets of code that collect and send data to a third party, often for tracking and analytics purposes. Tag management is a crucial practice for organizations aiming to streamline data collection, enhance marketing strategies, and improve website performance. Despite its benefits, managing tags can present several common challenges that can impact efficiency and accuracy. Below, we explore these challenges comprehensively.

One of the foremost challenges in managing tags is complexity. Websites typically use a wide array of tags from various vendors, such as Google Analytics, Facebook Pixels, and advertising networks. Each of these tags serves different purposes and requires specific configurations. Coordinating these tags and ensuring they do not conflict with one another can be a daunting task. Without a clear and organized approach, the cumulative effect of multiple tags can lead to performance issues, causing websites to slow down or even become unresponsive at times.

Closely related to complexity is the challenge of tag consistency and accuracy. Inaccurately implemented tags can result in faulty data collection, leading to misguided decision-making. For instance, a misplaced tag might record duplicate data or fail to capture crucial user interactions. Ensuring that all tags are correctly placed, structured, and tested for accuracy can be labor-intensive and requires continuous monitoring.

Another significant challenge is version control. As websites evolve and updates are pushed live, previously established tags may become obsolete or need adjustments to accommodate new site structures and functionalities. Manual updating of these tags can be error-prone, as even small changes in website code can disrupt the tag functionality. Without a consistent version control process, organizations might face difficulties in tracking changes, leading to inconsistencies in data collection over time.

Security and privacy concerns also pose challenges in managing tags. Tags, by their nature, involve the collection of user data, which can include sensitive information. Organizations must ensure compliance with data protection regulations such as GDPR, CCPA, and other local privacy laws. This requires tags to be configured in a manner that respects user consent choices and data minimization principles. Failing to do so can result in regulatory penalties and damage to brand reputation.

In high-traffic environments, managing the load and efficiency of tags is crucial. Tags that load synchronously can block the rendering of a webpage, frustrating users and increasing bounce rates. Asynchronous loading of tags, while generally mitigating this issue, still requires careful management to ensure that essential tags are prioritized over less critical ones. Poorly optimized tags can significantly degrade user experience and impact site performance metrics.

Inter-departmental coordination represents another logistical challenge in tag management. Organizations often have multiple stakeholders—including marketing, IT, and data analytics teams—each with specific needs and objectives regarding tag use. Achieving alignment between these departments is critical for an effective tag management strategy. A lack of clear communication channels and defined roles can lead to duplication of efforts, misaligned goals, and a fragmented approach to tag management.

One solution to many of these challenges is the use of Tag Management Systems (TMS), such as Google Tag Manager or Adobe Launch. While TMS can vastly simplify the process of managing tags by providing a centralized platform for implementation and updates, they are not without their own complexities. Organizations must invest in training and ongoing education to ensure that staff are proficient in using these systems. Additionally, there can be a learning curve associated with integrating and customizing a TMS to fit the specific needs of the organization.

Lastly, data governance is an underlying challenge that permeates all aspects of tag management. Establishing clear policies and procedures for tag implementation, monitoring, and auditing is essential. Organizations need to invest in continuous education and skills development to ensure that their teams remain adept at managing the ever-evolving landscape of digital data collection.

In conclusion, while managing tags is indispensable for modern data-driven decision-making, it is fraught with challenges ranging from complexity and accuracy to inter-departmental coordination and regulatory compliance. Addressing these challenges requires a holistic approach incorporating robust tools, clear communication, and ongoing education.

## 18.2 Overcoming Resistance to Tagging Initiatives

Resistance to tagging initiatives is a challenge often encountered in various settings, from corporate environments to educational institutions. Tagging initiatives, which involve categorizing and labeling content, data, or information for easier retrieval and organization, hold significant potential benefits. These benefits include enhanced searchability, better data management, and improved user experiences. However, the implementation of such initiatives can be met with skepticism, reluctance, and outright resistance from stakeholders. Understanding the sources of this resistance and developing strategies to overcome them are crucial for the successful adoption of tagging initiatives.

One of the primary sources of resistance is the perceived increase in workload. People often see tagging as an additional task that requires extra effort without immediate, tangible benefits. This perception is particularly prevalent among employees who already have full schedules and face high demands on their time. To address this concern, it is essential to clearly communicate the long-term benefits of tagging initiatives. Demonstrating how tagging can save time in the future—by making information retrieval faster and reducing redundant efforts—can help shift the perspective from short-term inconvenience to long-term efficiency.

Another common resistance stems from the lack of understanding about the purpose and importance of tagging. Stakeholders may not fully grasp how tagging can improve processes or why it is necessary. To counter this, comprehensive training and education are vital. Workshops, seminars, and hands-on training sessions can play a crucial role in bridging the knowledge gap. By educating individuals about the advantages of tagging, such as improved project management, enhanced collaboration, and streamlined workflows, they are more likely to appreciate its value and engage with the initiative willingly.

Cultural resistance can also pose a significant barrier. In some organizations, there is a strong adherence to traditional methods and a reluctance to adopt new technologies or practices. Overcoming this cultural inertia requires a multifaceted approach. Leadership plays a critical role in setting the tone and demonstrating commitment to the initiative. When employees see that their leaders are actively participating in and supporting tagging initiatives, they are more likely to follow suit. Additionally, identifying and involving early adopters—individuals who are enthusiastic about new technologies and can influence their peers—can create a ripple effect that encourages broader acceptance.

The complexity of the tagging system itself can also lead to resistance. If the system is perceived as too complicated or unintuitive, users may be discouraged from using it. Simplifying the tagging process is, therefore, essential. User-friendly interfaces, clear guidelines, and intuitive design can make the tagging system more accessible. Moreover, incorporating user feedback to continuously improve the system can ensure that it meets the needs and preferences of its users.

Resistance can also arise from concerns about data privacy and security. Employees may worry that tagging initiatives could expose sensitive information or lead to unauthorized access. Addressing these concerns transparently is crucial. Providing assurances through robust data protection measures, clear privacy policies, and transparent communication about how data will be used and protected can alleviate fears and build trust.

To successfully overcome resistance, it is also beneficial to adopt a phased approach to implementation. Introducing tagging initiatives gradually, rather than all at once, allows for adjustments based on feedback and helps to manage the impact on workflows. Starting with a pilot project or a small-scale implementation can provide valuable insights and serve as proof of concept. Success stories and positive outcomes from initial phases can be leveraged to build momentum and support for broader adoption.

Finally, recognizing and rewarding participation can significantly boost engagement. Acknowledgment of efforts, whether through formal recognition programs, incentives, or simple appreciation, can motivate individuals to embrace tagging initiatives. Celebrating successes and sharing positive experiences can reinforce the benefits and create a positive association with the initiative.

In conclusion, overcoming resistance to tagging initiatives requires a comprehensive and strategic approach. By addressing concerns about workload, providing education, fostering a supportive culture, simplifying the system, ensuring data security, adopting a phased implementation, and recognizing participation, organizations can effectively navigate resistance and achieve successful adoption of tagging initiatives. The long-term benefits of improved data management, enhanced collaboration, and increased efficiency make the effort worthwhile, paving the way for a more organized and productive environment.

# 18.3 Regulatory and Compliance Challenges in Tag Management

Navigating the regulatory and compliance landscape in tag management presents a crucial challenge for businesses that rely heavily on digital marketing and data analytics. As the volume of data generated by digital interactions grows, so does the complexity of managing that data in accordance with various international, federal, and state laws. Let's delve into some key regulatory and compliance challenges encountered in tag management.

First, privacy regulations such as the General Data Protection Regulation (GDPR) in the European Union and the California Consumer Privacy Act (CCPA) in the United States have a profound impact on how organizations handle data tagging. These laws mandate stringent guidelines for data collection, usage, and sharing, requiring businesses to obtain explicit consent from users before storing or processing their personal information. Failure to comply can result in hefty fines, making it imperative for organizations to review and update their tag management processes regularly.

A pivotal challenge within this domain is the need to ensure transparency and user consent. Tags are often used to track user behavior across websites, which can involve collecting sensitive personal information. Under GDPR, for example, businesses must provide a clear and comprehensible way for users to give or withdraw consent regarding which tags are operating on a given website. This often means implementing granular consent settings and regularly updating them to reflect changes in the regulatory environment or new tags introduced into the system.

Moreover, maintaining an accurate and up-to-date tag inventory poses another significant compliance challenge. Most websites utilize numerous third-party tags for various purposes, including advertising, analytics, and user experience optimization. Each of these tags carries its own set of data collection practices and privacy implications. Thus, organizations must continuously audit their tag inventories to ensure compliance with current regulations. This may involve identifying rogue or obsolete tags that could compromise user privacy or lead to data leakage.

Data governance also plays a critical role in tag management compliance. Organizations must establish and enforce policies for data handling and retention, particularly in light of stringent regulations like GDPR, which grants individuals the right to be forgotten. This means that tags must not only support data minimization principles—collecting only the data that is necessary for a specified purpose—but also ensure that data can be efficiently purged when it is no longer required or when a user requests its deletion.

Another intricate layer of the regulatory challenge is the management of cross-border data transfers. With tag management systems often processing data that can be transferred between different jurisdictions, businesses must be vigilant about adhering to international data protection laws. Provisions such as GDPR's Standard Contractual Clauses (SCCs) or the use of binding corporate rules (BCRs) are mechanisms through which organizations can legally transfer data across borders. Navigating these complex frameworks requires meticulous planning and often legal consultation to ensure full regulatory compliance.

Furthermore, the risk of vendor non-compliance is an issue that cannot be overlooked. Since tag management frequently involves third-party vendors, organizations must ensure that their partners adhere to the same rigorous compliance standards. This might involve conducting thorough due diligence, including regular assessments and audits of third-party vendors' privacy policies and security practices.

The dynamic nature of regulatory requirements adds another layer of complexity to tag management. Laws and regulations are continually evolving, often spurred by technological advancements and shifting public attitudes toward privacy. For instance, the adoption of cookie-less tracking technology or new browser privacy features can necessitate immediate changes in tag management practices. Businesses must stay agile and adaptable, keeping abreast of legislative developments and ensuring their tag management strategies are responsive to new regulatory demands.

Additionally, robust data security measures are vital in mitigating risks associated with tag management. Tags can be a vector for security vulnerabilities if not properly managed, posing potential risks such as data breaches or unauthorized data access. Ensuring that tags are correctly implemented, regularly updated, and safeguarded against potential threats is fundamental to maintaining compliance and protecting user data.

In conclusion, the regulatory and compliance challenges inherent in tag management are multifaceted and demand continual vigilance. Organizations must prioritize transparency, consent management, data governance, and security while staying informed about evolving regulations to effectively navigate this intricate landscape.

# 18.4 Strategies for Overcoming Tag Management Barriers

Navigating the intricacies of tag management can be daunting for many organizations. Executing an effective tag management strategy requires overcoming various barriers that impede the process. Here are several strategies that can help in overcoming these obstacles:

### 1. Understanding Tag Management Systems (TMS):

The first step in overcoming tag management barriers is developing a deep understanding of Tag Management Systems (TMS). Investing in training programs and educational resources for your team can empower them with the necessary knowledge to effectively implement and manage tags. Familiarize your team with different TMS platforms, their unique features, and best practices for efficient tag management.

### 2. Stakeholder Alignment:

Securing stakeholder buy-in is crucial. Often, resistance comes from within the organization due to lack of understanding or concerns over privacy and data security. Organizations need to educate stakeholders about the benefits of TMS, including improved website performance, enhanced data accuracy, and better marketing analytics. Demonstrating how TMS aligns with organizational goals will foster greater acceptance and smoother implementation.

### 3. Governance and Policy Development:

Establishing clear governance structures and policies for tag management is essential. This includes defining roles and responsibilities, creating protocols for tag deployment, and setting standards for tag usage and data collection. Governance ensures that all tags are implemented consistently and according to predefined rules, minimizing the risks of data leakage and compliance issues.

### 4. Collaboration Between Teams:

Collaboration between marketing, IT, and data analytics teams is vital for overcoming tag management barriers. Each of these departments has a stake in how tags are managed and deployed. Regular meetings and integrated workflows help in making sure that each team's needs and concerns are addressed, leading to a more cohesive and efficient tag management process.

### 5. Prioritization of Tags:

Cybellium - Google Tag Manager Certification

Not all tags are created equal. Prioritize tags based on their criticality to business objectives and their potential impact on website performance. Lower-priority tags can be deferred or scheduled for later deployment to minimize performance issues. This approach ensures that only essential tags are implemented first, maintaining the efficiency and efficacy of the site.

## 6. Use of Tag Audits:

Regular audits of existing tags help in identifying redundant or outdated tags that may be slowing down the website or compromising data quality. Tag audits should be conducted periodically to keep the tag ecosystem clean and efficient. Third-party tools can facilitate comprehensive tag audits and provide insights into potential areas for improvement.

## 7. Performance Monitoring:

Continuous monitoring of tag performance is crucial. Use analytics tools to track how tags affect website metrics such as load times, bounce rates, and overall user experience. Performance insights can guide decisions on whether certain tags need to be optimized, adjusted, or removed altogether.

## 8. Incremental Implementation:

Instead of rolling out a complete tag management overhaul at once, consider incremental implementation. Deploying tags in phases allows for better control and the ability to address issues promptly. This approach reduces risks and ensures stability throughout the transition process.

## 9. Enhanced Security Measures:

Tags can pose security risks if not managed properly. Employing robust security measures — such as encrypting data transmitted through tags and utilizing secure tag management platforms — can protect sensitive information from breaches. Regularly updating security protocols also helps in mitigating new threats.

## 10. Leveraging Automation:

Automating routine tag management tasks can significantly reduce manual intervention and errors. Automation tools can streamline the process of tag deployment, update, and removal, ensuring a more efficient and error-free tag management lifecycle.

## 11. Vendor Management:

Work closely with tag management vendors to understand the complete capabilities of their solutions. Vendors can provide tailored support, updates, and best practices that can enhance your tag management strategy. Regular communication ensures that your team is leveraging the most effective features of the TMS at your disposal.

## 12. Documentation and Knowledge Sharing:

Maintaining comprehensive documentation of the tag management processes ensures continuity, especially when there are staffing changes. Detailed guides, SOPs, and knowledge-sharing sessions can help new team members quickly get up to speed and ensure consistency in tag management practices.

## 13. Integration with Data Privacy Regulations:

Keeping abreast of local and international data privacy regulations, such as GDPR or CCPA, is crucial. Ensuring that your tag management practices are compliant with these regulations will protect your organization from legal repercussions and build trust with your users.

## 14. Regular Training:

Technology and best practices in tag management are constantly evolving. Regular training sessions can help your team stay current with the latest trends, tools, and techniques. Ongoing education will equip your team with the skills necessary to navigate the ever-changing landscape of tag management.

## 15. Troubleshooting Framework:

Developing a robust troubleshooting framework helps in quickly identifying and resolving issues related to tag deployment. This framework should include common problems, diagnostic tools, and step-by-step solutions to maintain smooth operations.

## 16. Review Competitor Strategies:

Analyzing the tag management strategies of competitors can provide insights and inspiration. Understanding how other organizations tackle similar challenges can inform your own strategies and help you avoid common pitfalls.

## 17. Custom Solutions:

Sometimes, the out-of-the-box solutions provided by TMS vendors might not meet all organizational needs. Working with vendors to develop custom solutions, or employing in-house developers to tailor tools to specific requirements, ensures that your tag management strategy is perfectly aligned with your business goals.

## 18. Feedback Loops:

Creating feedback loops where team members can report issues and suggest improvements fosters a culture of continuous improvement. Regular feedback sessions will help your team address new challenges promptly and refine your tag management strategy over time.

By implementing these strategies, organizations can effectively navigate the complexities of tag management, ensuring a streamlined, secure, and efficient process that ultimately supports broader business objectives.

# 19. Tags and Public Policy

Chapter 19 delves into the intricate relationship between tags and public policy, unraveling the layers of complexity that govern this dynamic interaction. As digital tagging systems become increasingly ubiquitous, their implications for privacy, surveillance, and regulatory frameworks demand rigorous examination. This chapter aims to illuminate the multifaceted nature of tags in the context of public policy, highlighting both the opportunities they present for enhanced governance and the challenges they pose for individual rights and societal norms. Through a critical analysis of case studies and theoretical frameworks, we will explore how policymakers grapple with the evolving technological landscape, striving to balance innovation with ethical considerations.

# 19.1 The Role of Government in Shaping Tag Regulations

Governmental regulation plays a critical role in the development and implementation of tag regulations across various industries. Tags—identifying labels often containing vital information pertaining to a product or service—are ubiquitous in the modern world. They provide details such as origin, material composition, usage instructions, warnings, and tracking information. This kind of information is essential not only for consumer protection but also for efficient market operations and regulatory compliance. Governments engage in shaping tag regulations to ensure public safety, environmental sustainability, fair trade practices, and to streamline the administrative needs of both businesses and bureaucrats.

Firstly, the government's primary concern is consumer protection. By setting stringent requirements for tags, regulatory bodies ensure that consumers are fully informed about the products they purchase. This is especially crucial for items that pose potential risks, such as pharmaceuticals, food, and electrical appliances. For instance, the U.S. Food and Drug Administration (FDA) has stringent guidelines for labeling pharmaceutical drugs, which include dosage instructions, possible side effects, and contraindications. Likewise, the U.S. Department of Agriculture (USDA) mandates specific labels for organic foods to guarantee that products meet established organic standards. Through these measures, governments act as gatekeepers of public health and safety.

Additionally, environmental protection is a significant aspect of governmental influence in tag regulations. Tags on various products, especially consumer electronics, chemicals, and automobiles, often include information about material composition and recycling instructions. Governments proactively legislate these disclosures to encourage recycling and responsible disposal, thereby reducing environmental pollution. For example, the European Union's Waste Electrical and Electronic Equipment (WEEE) directive mandates producers to provide clear instructions on the disposal and recycling of electronic goods. This ensures that hazardous materials like lead and mercury are safely disposed of, mitigating their potential impact on the environment.

Another key driver behind governmental regulation of tags is the promotion of fair trade practices. Tags serve as essential tools in ensuring that products meet specific standards, thereby facilitating transparent trade and protecting intellectual property rights. Governments enforce regulations that require tags to disclose country of origin, fair labor practices, and compliance with trade agreements. By doing so, they promote a level playing field for businesses and protect consumers from counterfeit and substandard goods. For instance, the

Cybellium - Google Tag Manager Certification

International Trade Administration (ITA) of the United States monitors labeling requirements to protect American businesses from unfair foreign competition.

Moreover, governments leverage tag regulations to assist in the efficient administration of various programs and tax regimes. Tags containing barcodes, QR codes, and RFID (Radio-frequency Identification) technology are instrumental in tracking products throughout the supply chain. By mandating the use of such tags, governments can better oversee imports, exports, and taxation. This is particularly relevant for high-value items like alcohol, tobacco, and luxury goods, where accurate tracking minimizes tax evasion and smuggling. For example, many governments use tax stamps on cigarette packs to verify that the appropriate taxes have been paid. This helps to curb illegal trade practices while ensuring revenue collection.

In conclusion, the role of government in shaping tag regulations is multifaceted and indispensable. From safeguarding public health and the environment to fostering fair trade practices and ensuring efficient administration, governmental involvement in tag regulation is pivotal. Regulatory bodies take painstaking measures to design and enforce these regulations, balancing the needs of consumers, businesses, and the broader society. As products continue to evolve and the market dynamics shift, the government's role in refining and updating tag regulations remains crucial in navigating the complexities of modern economies. Through robust and well-crafted tag regulations, governments not only protect and inform their citizens but also foster a more transparent, sustainable, and equitable marketplace.

# 19.2 Public-Private Partnerships in Tag Management

Public-Private Partnerships (PPPs) in tag management represent a collaborative approach between government entities and private sector organizations to streamline, enhance, and innovate tag management systems. These systems are pivotal for a myriad of applications, including transportation tolling, access control, and even digital marketing and data collection. By leveraging the strengths and resources of both the public and private sectors, these partnerships aim to deliver higher efficiency, improved technological integration, and enhanced user experiences.

## Definition and Structure of Tag Management Systems

Tag management systems (TMS) are platforms or protocols that facilitate the collection, organization, and utilization of data generated by tags. Tags, in this context, refer to markers or identifiers that can be physical (e.g., RFID tags used for toll collection) or digital (e.g., tracking pixels used on websites). These systems are crucial in environments where large volumes of data need to be accurately tracked, processed, and acted upon in real time.

## The Role of Public Entities

Public entities, often governmental or regulatory bodies, are predominantly responsible for establishing the frameworks and infrastructures necessary for tag management systems, particularly in public services such as transportation and security. They bring to the table a deep understanding of regulatory requirements, standardized protocols, and a focus on public interest and accessibility. These organizations often manage and maintain the foundational infrastructure, ensuring compliance with safety standards and supporting widespread, equitable access to the services enabled by tag management systems.

## Contributions of Private Sector Partners

Private sector entities contribute by injecting innovation, technological expertise, and capital investments into the development and maintenance of TMS. These organizations frequently have access to cutting-edge technologies, project management skills, and efficiencies driven by competition and profit motives. Private companies can rapidly adapt to emerging trends, such as advancements in IoT (Internet of Things), big data analytics, and AI (Artificial Intelligence), which can significantly enhance the functionality and responsiveness of tag management systems.

Cybellium - Google Tag Manager Certification

## Case Studies in Transportation and Tolling

One of the most prominent areas where PPPs in tag management have been successful is in transportation, particularly tolling systems. Take, for example, the collaboration between state governments and private toll operators in managing electronic toll collection systems. In the United States, systems like E-ZPass have revolutionized highway tolling by reducing congestion and easing the payment process for drivers. These systems use RFID tags and readers to automate toll collection, requiring significant investment in technology and infrastructure that many public entities cannot manage alone.

By partnering with private firms, governments can ensure robust, state-of-the-art systems are put in place. The private partners undertake the development and ongoing management of these systems in exchange for a share of the collected toll revenue. This model ensures that the public sector can provide an essential service without bearing the full financial and operational burdens.

## Digital Marketing and Data Analytics

In the digital realm, tag management systems are crucial for collecting and analyzing user data, which can inform decision-making processes and strategy formulations in various industries. Here, public-private partnerships can ensure that data collection and usage comply with stringent privacy and security regulations. For example, European countries have worked with private firms to implement GDPR-compliant tag management solutions that respect user privacy while enabling businesses to harness the power of data analytics.

## Benefits of Public-Private Synergy

The synergy between public oversight and private innovation in tag management facilitates enhanced adaptability, better user experiences, and improved data accuracy. Public entities benefit from reduced financial burdens and access to innovative solutions, while private entities can capitalize on the extensive reach and regulatory support of public systems. This collaboration also promotes transparency, accountability, and trust among users who may be wary of data privacy and misuse.

## Future Prospects and Challenges

Looking ahead, the scope of PPPs in tag management is likely to expand with the advent of smart cities, advanced transportation systems, and increasingly sophisticated digital ecosystems. However, these partnerships will need to address several challenges, including interoperability of diverse systems, data security concerns, and equitable access to technology. Ensuring that both parties remain aligned in their goals and responsibilities will be crucial to the ongoing success of these collaborative efforts.

In conclusion, Public-Private Partnerships in tag management hold immense potential to revolutionize how data is gathered, processed, and utilized across various sectors. By combining the public sector's strategic oversight with the private sector's technological acumen, these partnerships can deliver efficient, user-friendly, and secure tag management systems that serve the needs of modern society.

# 19.3 Navigating Regulatory Changes in Tag Management

Navigating regulatory changes in tag management is a multifaceted challenge that every digital marketer must grapple with. With the ever-evolving landscape of data privacy laws and digital regulations, staying compliant while ensuring optimal performance is a dynamic and often complex endeavor. Effective tag management is crucial for tracking, analytics, and various marketing activities, but it must be balanced with strict adherence to regulatory requirements to avoid legal repercussions and maintain consumer trust.

The General Data Protection Regulation (GDPR) in Europe, the California Consumer Privacy Act (CCPA) in the United States, and other similar regulations globally have significantly impacted how businesses manage tags, cookies, and online tracking. These regulations necessitate a reconsideration of data processing practices, particularly regarding user consent, data storage, and usage transparency.

One of the first steps in navigating these changes is conducting a comprehensive audit of current tag management practices. This audit should identify all tags and associated data flows within the digital ecosystem. Understanding what data is collected, how it's processed, where it's stored, and who has access to it is fundamental. This initial assessment provides the foundation for making necessary adjustments to comply with regulatory requirements.

Once the audit is complete, the focus shifts to obtaining explicit user consent for data collection and processing, a cornerstone of regulations like GDPR and CCPA. Implementing consent management platforms (CMPs) can facilitate this process. CMPs are designed to handle consent capture and storage, ensuring that users are fully informed about what data is being collected and how it will be used, allowing them to exercise their rights to opt-in or opt-out.

In practice, getting user consent affects how tags are managed. Tag management platforms must be configured to deploy tags conditionally based on the user's consent. This means that if a user declines consent, tracking tags must be disabled or adjusted accordingly. Failure to comply can result in substantial fines and damage to a brand's reputation.

Beyond consent, regulatory changes demand enhanced transparency in data practices. Businesses must clearly articulate their data policies in accessible privacy notices and ensure that these notices are readily available to users. Consistency between declared policies and actual practices is not just recommended but legally required. Regular reviews of privacy notices against operational practices can help maintain this alignment and ensure ongoing compliance.

Data minimization is another critical aspect. Regulations emphasize collecting only the data necessary for specific purposes and retaining it only as long as required. Tag management systems should be configured to adhere to these principles, ensuring that data collection is limited to what is justified and needed. Moreover, businesses should establish protocols for regular data purges to remove outdated or unnecessary information.

Considering cross-border data flows is also essential for regulatory compliance. Tags and associated data often traverse multiple jurisdictions, each with its regulatory framework. Businesses must be cognizant of international data transfer laws and ensure that appropriate safeguards, such as Standard Contractual Clauses (SCCs) or Binding Corporate Rules (BCRs), are in place when transferring data outside the region of origin.

Another aspect to consider is the robustness and security of data storage and processing. Regulatory frameworks mandate that collected data be kept secure against breaches and unauthorized access. This involves implementing state-of-the-art encryption, access control, and regular security audits. Tag management systems should work in concert with broader IT security policies to ensure that all aspects of data handling are secure.

Finally, maintaining a responsive approach to regulatory changes is critical. Laws and regulations are not static; they evolve. Staying current with legislative developments and industry best practices requires a commitment to continuous learning and adaptation. Establishing a dedicated compliance team or working with legal advisors specializing in digital data regulations can help proactively manage changes and integrate them into the tag management strategy efficiently.

In conclusion, navigating regulatory changes in tag management is a continuous and dynamic process that requires diligence, foresight, and adaptability. By conducting thorough audits, implementing robust consent mechanisms, maintaining transparency, minimizing data collection, ensuring cross-border compliance, securing data, and staying informed about regulatory developments, businesses can manage their tags effectively while adhering to the complex web of global data regulations. This balance not only ensures compliance but also fosters consumer trust and strengthens brand integrity in an increasingly privacy-conscious world.

# 19.4 Challenges in Aligning Tagging with Public Policy

Aligning tagging with public policy presents a multifaceted array of challenges that can be understood from technological, societal, regulatory, and ethical perspectives. The integration of tagging systems into any public policy framework must address these complexities to ensure effective and equitable implementation.

From a technological standpoint, tagging systems rely on accurate data collection and advanced algorithms to categorize and label information. However, the integrity of this data can be compromised by issues such as data breaches, inaccuracies, and biases. Robust data governance practices are essential but difficult to maintain across diverse and dynamic datasets. Additionally, the rapid rate of technological change presents another layer of difficulty. Policymakers must create flexible frameworks that can adapt to advancements in tagging technologies while ensuring compliance with current standards.

Societal challenges are equally significant. Tagging systems can inadvertently reinforce societal prejudices and inequalities. For example, an algorithm trained on biased data may perpetuate those biases in its categorization, leading to discriminatory practices. This raises concerns around fairness and accountability. Ensuring that tagging systems are transparent and inclusive can be challenging, necessitating collaborative efforts with diverse stakeholders to mitigate biases. Moreover, public awareness and understanding of tagging technologies are often limited, which can lead to mistrust and resistance. Campaigns aimed at educating the public about the benefits and limitations of tagging are crucial but require substantial resources and strategic communication.

Regulatory challenges involve the creation and enforcement of laws that govern tagging systems. As these systems often operate across multiple jurisdictions, harmonizing regulations to achieve consistency and fairness is complex. Policymakers must tackle the balance between encouraging innovation and protecting public interests. Privacy laws, for instance, are central to tagging practices, as tags often involve personal data. Compliance with regulations such as the General Data Protection Regulation (GDPR) in Europe requires meticulous attention to data privacy and security. Moreover, striking the right balance between transparency and protection of proprietary information poses a legal conundrum that requires nuanced approaches.

Ethical considerations are perhaps the most profound challenges in aligning tagging with public policy. There is an inherent tension between the potential benefits of tagging systems—such as increased efficiency and better resource allocation—and the risks they pose to individual rights and social equity. Ethical concerns revolve around consent, autonomy, and the potential for abuse. For example, individuals should have control over how their data is tagged and used, but implementing comprehensive consent mechanisms can be daunting. Additionally, the use of tagging for surveillance purposes can lead to significant ethical breaches, raising concerns about autonomy and freedom. Policymakers must establish ethical guidelines that explicitly address these potential harms while promoting the responsible use of tagging technologies.

Thus, the path to aligning tagging with public policy is fraught with challenges, but it is not without potential solutions. Engaging a multidisciplinary approach that includes technologists, sociologists, legal experts, and ethicists can pave the way for more holistic and effective policies. Continuous dialogue with the public and transparent practices can foster trust and acceptance. Developing adaptive regulatory frameworks that can evolve with technological advancements while maintaining robust ethical standards is crucial for sustainable integration of tagging systems into public policy.

In conclusion, the alignment of tagging with public policy requires careful navigation of technological, societal, regulatory, and ethical landscapes. By addressing these multifaceted challenges through inclusive, adaptive, and transparent approaches, policymakers can harness the benefits of tagging technologies while safeguarding public interests and promoting social equity.

# 20. Human Capital in Tag Management

In the evolving landscape of digital marketing, the strategic deployment of tags—small pieces of code inserted into a website's source code—ensures the collection of valuable data and the effective execution of marketing campaigns. However, the technology and tools used to manage these tags are only as powerful as the people behind them. Human capital plays an irreplaceable role in the efficacy of tag management systems (TMS). Expertise in TMS not only involves technical knowledge and skills but also strategic thinking and alignment with overarching business goals. In this chapter, we delve into how the fusion of skilled professionals and sophisticated technology drives successful tag management. From the technical proficiency required to implement and debug tags, to the governance and oversight needed to maintain data integrity and privacy, we will explore the myriad ways human talent augments tag management processes. Understanding this dynamic will provide you with invaluable insights into optimizing both your human and technological resources, paving the way for superior data-driven decision-making and campaign execution.

## 20.1 Building Expertise in Tag Management

To develop a comprehensive understanding of tag management, it is crucial to first capture the essence of what tags are and how they function within the digital landscape. Tags serve as snippets of code embedded in a website's HTML or JavaScript, enabling the collection and transmission of data to various marketing and analytics platforms. This data can then be used for a multitude of purposes, including tracking user behavior, optimizing advertising campaigns, and improving overall site performance.

The journey to building expertise in tag management begins with mastering the foundational concepts and tools associated with it. One of the essential tools in this realm is a Tag Management System (TMS), such as Google Tag Manager (GTM), Adobe Launch, or Tealium. These tools facilitate the organization and deployment of tags across a website without the need for constant updates to the site's codebase, thereby streamlining the process and lowering dependency on developers.

Understanding how a TMS operates is a fundamental step in becoming proficient. A TMS usually comprises three main components: containers, tags, and triggers. Containers serve as the primary holding structure that houses various tags and their corresponding triggers. Tags are the code snippets that collect and relay data, while triggers determine the conditions under which tags are fired. A deep understanding of these components and how they interact is crucial for efficient tag management.

Structured learning and hands-on experience go hand in hand to gain a thorough understanding. Online courses, tutorials, and certification programs offered by respective TMS providers are immensely helpful. For instance, the Google Tag Manager Fundamentals course provides a guided introduction to GTM, laying the groundwork for more advanced learning. Additionally, official documentation and community forums can be indispensable resources for troubleshooting and advanced tips.

A proficient tag manager must also be adept at debugging and testing tags before they go live. Debugging tools, like the GTM Preview mode, enable the visualization of tag firing and the examination of data layers. Mastery of these tools ensures that tags are functioning correctly and collecting the intended data. Critical thinking and an analytical mindset are necessary to identify discrepancies and rectify issues promptly.

Moreover, a strong grasp of JavaScript and HTML can greatly enhance one's capabilities in tag management. Custom tags and triggers often require scripting skills for complex conditions and data processing. Proficiency in JavaScript not only aids in the creation of custom tags but also in understanding and manipulating the data layer—a structured object that holds data passed between the TMS and the website.

In the broader context, integration with other marketing and analytics platforms is a key area of expertise for tag managers. Understanding how tags work in conjunction with tools like Google Analytics, Facebook Pixel, and other third-party services is vital. This includes configuring tags to capture specific events, such as user interactions, page views, and conversions, and ensuring the accurate transmission of this data to the relevant platforms.

Data privacy and compliance are increasingly significant aspects of tag management. Familiarity with regulations like the General Data Protection Regulation (GDPR) and the California Consumer Privacy Act (CCPA) is crucial. Ensuring that tags respect user consent and data privacy protocols is an ethical and legal responsibility. Setting up consent management platforms (CMPs) and configuring tags to trigger based on user consent are necessary skills in today's regulatory environment.

In summary, building expertise in tag management involves a combination of theoretical knowledge and practical application. From understanding the basic components of a Tag Management System and mastering debugging tools to acquiring scripting skills and ensuring compliance with data privacy regulations, a diverse set of capabilities is essential. Continuous learning, supported by a robust community and evolving tools, is vital for maintaining and advancing one's proficiency in this dynamic field.

## 20.2 Developing Leadership in Tag Strategies

Effective leadership is a cornerstone of successful organizations, and developing leadership within tag strategies is a process that requires deliberate planning, strategic thinking, and an understanding of the dynamic roles different leaders play within these frameworks. Tag strategies, often employed in digital marketing and information systems, involve the use of tags to categorize, track, and manage data efficiently. The complexity and technological sophistication of these strategies necessitate strong leadership to ensure they are implemented effectively and yield the desired results.

Leadership development in this context involves a multi-faceted approach: understanding the technical aspects of tag strategies, fostering collaboration among team members, and encouraging innovation and adaptability. A leader must be both a technologist and a strategist, capable of bridging the gap between data management and broader organizational goals.

The first step in cultivating leadership in tag strategies is ensuring that leaders possess a thorough understanding of the technical details. This includes familiarity with various tagging technologies, data analytics tools, and the ability to interpret data accurately. Leaders must also be aware of the potential pitfalls, such as data privacy concerns and the importance of maintaining data accuracy. Investing in continuous education and training for leaders is crucial, as the technology landscape is constantly evolving.

Beyond technical proficiency, effective leaders must be adept at managing people and processes. This involves setting clear goals, defining roles and responsibilities, and fostering a culture of accountability. In tag strategies, collaboration is key, as the process often involves cross-functional teams, including IT, marketing, and data analytics departments. A leader must facilitate communication and cooperation between these teams to ensure the smooth implementation of tagging initiatives.

To encourage collaboration, leaders should adopt an inclusive approach, involving team members in decision-making processes and valuing their input. This helps to build a sense of ownership and commitment among team members, which is vital for the success of tag strategies. Regular meetings, workshops, and brainstorming sessions can provide platforms for team members to share ideas, discuss challenges, and develop solutions collectively.

Another important aspect of leadership in tag strategies is innovation. The digital landscape is constantly changing, and leaders must be open to exploring new technologies and methodologies. This requires a mindset that embraces change and encourages experimentation. Leaders should foster an environment where team members feel comfortable taking calculated risks and learning from failures. By promoting a culture of continuous improvement and innovation, leaders can ensure that their tag strategies remain effective and up-to-date.

Adaptability is another critical characteristic of effective leaders in this field. The rapid pace of technological advancements means that tag strategies must be flexible and scalable. Leaders must be able to pivot quickly in response to new developments, such as changes in consumer behavior, regulatory updates, or advancements in technology. This requires a proactive approach, continually monitoring the digital landscape and making adjustments as necessary.

Mentorship and succession planning are also vital components of leadership development in tag strategies. Experienced leaders should take the time to mentor junior team members, sharing their knowledge and expertise. This not only helps to build a stronger, more capable team but also ensures continuity within the organization. Succession planning involves identifying and training potential future leaders, ensuring that the organization is well-prepared for any transitions in leadership.

In conclusion, developing leadership in tag strategies is a complex but essential endeavor for any organization that relies on data-driven decision-making. By focusing on technical proficiency, fostering collaboration, encouraging innovation, being adaptable, and investing in mentorship and succession planning, organizations can cultivate leaders who are capable of navigating the intricacies of tag strategies and driving their teams towards success. Effective leadership in this area not only enhances the efficiency and accuracy of data management but also significantly contributes to the overall strategic goals of the organization.

# 20.3 Talent Management and Development in Tag Teams

The concept of talent management and development within the context of tag teams is an intricate and multifaceted endeavor, integral to the success and longevity of any professional wrestling organization. Tag teams, by their nature, offer unique dynamics that differ from singles competition, requiring specific attention to nurturing and honing the abilities and relationships of the performers involved.

Tag team wrestling is a specialized form of the sport, where the focus shifts from individual prowess to collective strategy and synergy. It requires a harmonious blend of skills, mutual understanding, and seamless cooperation between partners. The developmental phase for tag teams often starts with scouting and recruitment, where talent scouts identify promising individuals whose attributes and personas could complement one another in a team setting.

Once potential team members are identified, the training regime becomes critical. This often begins at developmental territories or performance centers, where wrestlers undergo rigorous physical training, technical skill enhancement, and psychological conditioning. However, for tag teams, there are additional layers of preparation. Wrestlers must learn to synchronize their moves, develop fluent in-ring communication, and understand each other's strengths and weaknesses intimately. This synchronization is not just limited to their wrestling techniques but extends to their entrance routines, promos, and overall character presentation.

Character development and storytelling are pivotal components of talent management within tag teams. A tag team must resonate with the audience, having a coherent backstory and distinct persona that fans can connect with. This involves creative collaboration between the wrestlers, writers, and producers. They must develop a compelling narrative that not only showcases their unity and chemistry but also defines their feuds and alliances. The evolution of their characters should reflect their growth as a team, allowing the audience to invest emotionally in their journey.

Promos and mic skills are another critical aspect. In tag teams, it is not just about individual charisma but how well the members can interact on the microphone, engage with the crowd, and sell their story. Effective communication between team members is essential for creating riveting and memorable promos that can elevate their status within the organization.

In-ring psychology and storytelling also play a crucial role in talent development. Tag team matches are inherently different from singles matches, often involving more complex booking arrangements, such as frequent tags, tandem moves, and the dramatic dynamics of isolation and comeback sequences. Wrestlers must master the art of tag team psychology to maintain the flow and excitement of their matches. This includes developing signature tandem moves, understanding when to build tension through near falls, and executing high spots that highlight their cohesiveness.

The chemistry between tag team partners cannot be overstated. Wrestling organizations often conduct team-building exercises and allow for ample time for partners to bond outside the ring. This could involve shared travel schedules, rooming arrangements on the road, and even social activities designed to strengthen their personal connections. A deep-seated trust and understanding can often translate into improved in-ring performance, as partners can anticipate each other's moves and reactions, making their sequences smoother and more believable.

In addition to the direct involvement of wrestlers, the role of coaches and mentors is paramount. Experienced veterans who have thrived in tag team wrestling can offer invaluable insights and guidance. They can share strategies, provide constructive feedback, and instill important values such as teamwork, discipline, and perseverance.

Lastly, continuous evaluation and feedback are integral to the development process. Regular performance reviews, both in training settings and after live events, help wrestlers identify areas for improvement. Constructive criticism from peers, trainers, and management allows tag teams to refine their skills and adapt to the ever-evolving landscape of professional wrestling.

In conclusion, talent management and development in tag teams involve a holistic approach that encompasses physical training, character development, in-ring psychology, and personal chemistry. It is a meticulous process that requires collaboration, creativity, and dedication from the wrestlers and the organization. By investing in these areas, wrestling promotions can cultivate dynamic and compelling tag teams that captivate audiences and contribute significantly to the success of their brand.

# 20.4 The Role of Education and Training in Tagging Success

Education and training play a pivotal role in ensuring the successful implementation and effectiveness of tagging systems in various fields, including wildlife research, supply chain management, and healthcare. As technology advances, the complexity and sophistication of tagging equipment and techniques have increased, necessitating a comprehensive understanding and skill set among practitioners. Effective education and training programs are crucial in equipping individuals with the knowledge and capabilities to maximize the potential of tagging systems.

In wildlife research, for instance, tagging animals with electronic collars or passive integrated transponder (PIT) tags allows scientists to monitor animal movements, behavior, and population dynamics. Proper education on the biological implications and ethical considerations of tagging is essential. Researchers must be trained to handle animals safely and humanely, minimizing stress and ensuring the animals' welfare. Training programs could include theoretical knowledge about animal biology and behavior, as well as practical sessions that teach how to deploy and maintain the tags effectively. Misapplication or mishandling of tags due to inadequate training can lead to injury or increased mortality rates among tagged animals, thereby compromising research integrity and ethical standards.

In supply chain management, Radio Frequency Identification (RFID) tags and barcodes have revolutionized inventory tracking, reducing errors and improving efficiency. Education and training programs for personnel in supply chain roles are necessary to ensure the correct implementation and management of these technologies. Employees need to understand how to read, interpret, and utilize the data captured by tags to make informed decisions about inventory control, logistics, and resource allocation. Training should cover both the technical aspects of the tagging systems, such as software usage and hardware maintenance, and the analytical skills required to leverage the data for operational improvements. Comprehensive training can lead to a more streamlined supply chain, reducing costs and enhancing productivity.

Healthcare is another sector where tagging systems, such as RFID wristbands for patient identification, have become increasingly prevalent. Proper education and training ensure that healthcare professionals can correctly apply and read these tags, thus avoiding potentially life-threatening mistakes. For instance, accurate patient identification is crucial to verify patient records, administer correct treatments, and avoid medical errors. Training healthcare providers in the use and troubleshooting of RFID systems, alongside education on data privacy and ethical practices, can significantly enhance patient safety and care quality.

Furthermore, the Internet of Things (IoT) has expanded the applications of tagging systems by connecting tagged objects and devices to the internet, enabling real-time monitoring and data analytics. As IoT devices proliferate, there is a growing need for specialized education and training programs to prepare professionals to manage and secure these interconnected systems. Cybersecurity, data analysis, and IoT infrastructure management are key areas of knowledge that need to be addressed in training programs. By fostering expertise in these areas, organizations can protect sensitive data, optimize the performance of their tagging systems, and prevent cyber threats.

In conclusion, the role of education and training in tagging success cannot be overstated. Whether in wildlife research, supply chain management, healthcare, or IoT applications, well-structured educational programs and comprehensive training are essential to ensure that tagging systems are implemented effectively and ethically. By investing in education and training, organizations can empower their personnel to utilize tagging technologies to their fullest potential, thereby achieving better outcomes and advancing their respective fields. The continuous evolution of tagging technologies underscores the need for ongoing education and skill development to keep pace with new advancements and challenges.

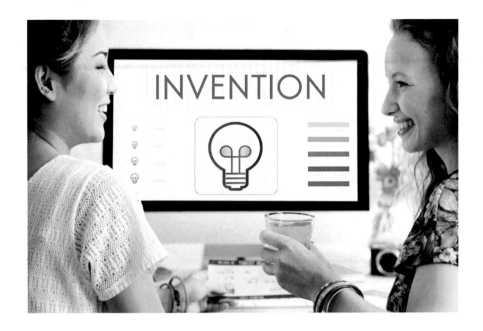

# 21. Innovation in Tag Management

Navigating the evolving landscape of digital marketing requires a robust understanding of a multitude of tools and strategies. Among these, tag management systems have emerged as a keystone in the architecture of modern analytics and marketing efforts. As the digital ecosystem becomes increasingly complex, the demand for sophisticated, flexible, and scalable tag management solutions has grown exponentially.

This chapter delves into the innovative strides being made in the realm of tag management. We will explore how advanced technologies and novel approaches are reshaping the way businesses deploy and manage tags. By examining cutting-edge features and integrations, this chapter aims to provide a comprehensive understanding of how innovation is driving efficiency, accuracy, and enhanced user experiences.

Through case studies, expert insights, and detailed analyses, readers will gain valuable knowledge on the latest trends and best practices in tag management. Whether you are looking to optimize your current system or implement a new one, this chapter will serve as a critical resource in leveraging the full potential of tag management innovation.

# 21.1 Leveraging Innovation for Tag Success

In today's hyper-competitive market, leveraging innovation for success is not only desirable but imperative. Whether in technology, healthcare, finance, or any other sector, innovation serves as a differentiator that can propel businesses to new heights. By strategically implementing innovative ideas, companies can solve complex problems, create unique value propositions, and stay ahead of the competition.

At its core, leveraging innovation involves a multi-faceted approach that addresses both internal and external factors. Internally, it requires fostering a culture that encourages creativity, experimentation, and risk-taking. Companies need to cultivate an environment where employees feel empowered to think outside the box and are not afraid to propose and test new ideas. This culture shift often starts from the top, with leadership not only endorsing but actively participating in innovative endeavors. By removing bureaucratic barriers and providing the necessary resources for innovation—such as time, funding, and infrastructure—companies can unlock their workforce's full creative potential.

Externally, leveraging innovation necessitates a keen sense of market dynamics and customer needs. Companies must maintain a pulse on market trends, emerging technologies, and competitive activities. Tools such as market research, customer feedback loops, and data analytics are invaluable for gaining insights into consumer behavior and identifying unmet needs. By staying attuned to these external factors, companies can more effectively anticipate changes and adapt their strategies accordingly.

One successful approach to leveraging innovation is through open innovation, which involves collaborating with external partners—such as startups, universities, and even competitors—to co-create solutions. This model expands the scope of potential ideas and resources available for innovation. It breaks down traditional silos and allows for cross-pollination of ideas, making it easier to bring new products or services to market faster. Companies like Procter & Gamble and IBM have adopted this strategy to great effect, tapping into external R&D capabilities to complement their in-house efforts.

In addition, the implementation of advanced technologies such as artificial intelligence (AI), blockchain, and the Internet of Things (IoT) can provide significant innovative breakthroughs. AI, for instance, can enhance decision-making processes, optimize supply chains, and deliver personalized customer experiences. Blockchain offers the potential for increased transparency, traceability, and security, which can be particularly beneficial for industries like finance and supply chain management. IoT can create smarter products and services that offer real-time insights and enhanced functionalities, thereby improving overall customer satisfaction.

To ensure that innovation efforts translate into tangible success, it is crucial to have a robust execution plan. This involves setting clear objectives, milestones, and key performance indicators (KPIs) to track progress and measure outcomes. Agile methodologies, which prioritize iterative development and constant feedback, can be particularly effective in managing innovative projects. By breaking down initiatives into smaller, manageable tasks and continuously refining them based on stakeholder feedback, companies can reduce risks and enhance the likelihood of successful implementation.

Moreover, leveraging innovation requires an alignment of organizational strategies and resources. Companies need to ensure that their innovation strategies are in sync with their overall business goals. This alignment involves careful planning and coordination across various departments, from R&D and marketing to legal and finance. By creating cross-functional teams that bring together diverse expertise and perspectives, companies can ensure that innovative solutions are not only creative but also feasible and scalable.

Metrics also play a crucial role in leveraging innovation. While traditional financial metrics like ROI are important, they may not always capture the full value of innovative efforts, especially in the early stages. Non-traditional metrics such as customer engagement, speed to market, and patent filings can provide a more nuanced view of an innovation's impact. Tracking these indicators can help companies refine their strategies, allocate resources more effectively, and ultimately achieve long-term success.

In conclusion, leveraging innovation is a comprehensive strategy that involves both fostering a creative internal culture and staying attuned to external market dynamics. By embracing open innovation, adopting advanced technologies, executing robust plans, aligning organizational strategies, and utilizing nuanced metrics, companies can not only innovate but do so in a way that drives sustained success.

## 21.2 Innovative Approaches to Tag Management

In the rapidly evolving digital landscape, efficient tag management is critical for website operations, marketing performance, and data analysis. The traditional methods of manually adding and updating tags not only consume valuable time but also increase the risk of human error, which can lead to malfunctioning pages, inaccurate data collection, and missed opportunities for business growth. Consequently, innovative approaches to tag management have emerged to address these challenges and enhance overall performance.

One notable innovation in this domain is the development of tag management systems (TMS). These platforms serve as centralized hubs for implementing, monitoring, and managing website tags without the need for constant coding intervention. By utilizing a TMS, organizations can gain significant agility in updates and tag deployments. Industry leaders such as Google Tag Manager, Adobe Launch, and Tealium iQ provide robust solutions that allow digital marketing teams to operate more autonomously from IT departments.

A more advanced approach within TMS is the use of server-side tag management. Unlike client-side tagging that runs scripts in the user's browser, server-side tagging processes data on a server before transmitting it to marketing and analytics tools. This method offers enhanced data security, improved site performance, and reduced risk of ad blockers interfering with data collection. Companies are exploring server-side tagging to create faster, more reliable systems, which is crucial for high-traffic websites and applications.

Another groundbreaking technique is the integration of machine learning and artificial intelligence within tag management systems. These tools can automate routine processes, detect anomalies, and optimize tag configurations based on performance metrics. By leveraging AI, businesses can ensure that tags are always functioning correctly and collecting the most relevant data, thereby improving targeting and personalization efforts.

Automation also extends to the deployment of tags using continuous integration and continuous deployment (CI/CD) pipelines. Employing DevOps practices in tag management allows for seamless and rapid updates, minimizing downtime and ensuring that marketing initiatives can react in real-time to changing market conditions. This integration facilitates a more cohesive strategy between marketing and development teams, driving efficiency and innovation.

The concept of event-driven tag management is another revolutionary approach in this space. Traditional tags are often static and limited in scope, triggering only under predefined conditions. Event-driven tagging, however, responds dynamically to user interactions and behaviors throughout their journey. This method enhances personalization by capturing more granular data points, leading to richer insights and more tailored marketing strategies. Tools like Segment and mParticle are at the forefront of event-driven tag management, offering brands the ability to refine their customer experiences continuously.

Privacy and compliance have become paramount concerns in the digital ecosystem, leading to the advent of consent management platforms (CMPs) integrated with TMS. These solutions ensure that data collection complies with regulations such as GDPR and CCPA, enabling users to manage their consent preferences transparently. By incorporating CMPs, companies can build trust with their users while maintaining robust data governance practices.

Moreover, the rise of container tags represents a significant leap in streamlined tag management. Container tags act as a single tag encompassing multiple individual tags, simplifying deployment and maintenance processes. This approach reduces overhead, as fewer code snippets need to be managed and executed, thereby improving page loading times and overall site performance.

Finally, multi-environment support within TMS allows businesses to test and validate tags in various staging environments before deploying them live. This feature mitigates risks associated with incorrect tag implementations and ensures that any issues can be identified and resolved preemptively. Multi-environment testing is especially valuable for large organizations with complex digital infrastructures, as it enables a controlled and systematic approach to tag management.

In conclusion, innovative approaches to tag management are transforming the digital marketing landscape by enhancing efficiency, accuracy, and adaptability. Through the implementation of sophisticated TMS platforms, server-side tagging, machine learning integrations, CI/CD pipelines, event-driven strategies, and robust privacy measures, businesses can effectively navigate the complexities of the modern digital ecosystem. Embracing these advancements ensures that organizations not only optimize their digital strategies but also stay ahead in a competitive market.

## 21.3 The Role of R&D in Advancing Tag Practices

Research and Development (R&D) plays a pivotal role in advancing tagging practices, especially in the context of data management, digital marketing, and technology innovation. The concept of tagging involves the assignment of metadata to various types of digital content, which can significantly enhance the accessibility, organization, and relevance of information. R&D initiatives are fundamental in evolving these practices, enabling more sophisticated, efficient, and accurate tagging systems.

First and foremost, one of the key contributions of R&D in tagging practices is the development of advanced algorithms. Traditional methods of tagging relied heavily on manual input, where human operators would assign tags based on predetermined categories. While effective to an extent, this method is fraught with limitations, such as human error and inconsistency. Through the continuous efforts of R&D, sophisticated machine learning algorithms have been created. These algorithms can automatically analyze enormous swathes of data and assign tags with remarkable accuracy. Using natural language processing (NLP) techniques, these algorithms can understand context, semantics, and even sentiment, making the tagging process not only faster but also significantly more precise.

Moreover, R&D efforts have led to the integration of artificial intelligence (AI) and deep learning technologies into tagging systems. AI-driven tagging systems can learn and adapt over time, improving the accuracy and relevancy of tags with each iteration. These systems are capable of identifying patterns and correlations that might not be immediately evident to human analysts. For instance, in the realm of digital marketing, AI can tag user-generated content based on trends and behaviors, enabling more personalized and targeted marketing strategies. This level of sophistication in tagging practices is only possible through ongoing R&D efforts in AI and deep learning.

Another significant area where R&D has advanced tagging practices is in the realm of interoperability and standardization. In a landscape where data is shared across various platforms and systems, the lack of standardized tagging practices can lead to fragmentation and inefficiency. R&D initiatives often focus on developing universal tagging standards and protocols, ensuring that tags are consistent and interoperable across different systems. This not only streamlines data management processes but also ensures that information can be seamlessly shared and integrated, enhancing overall efficiency.

Furthermore, R&D also plays a crucial role in enhancing the user experience associated with tagging systems. User-friendly interfaces and intuitive tagging frameworks are the result of extensive research into human-computer interaction (HCI). By understanding how users interact with tagging systems and identifying common pain points, R&D teams can develop solutions that are both efficient and easy to use. This ultimately leads to higher adoption rates and more effective utilization of tagging systems across various user demographics.

In addition to technical advancements, R&D also contributes to the ethical and regulatory aspects of tagging practices. As tagging systems become more advanced, issues related to privacy, data security, and ethical usage of data become increasingly pertinent. R&D efforts in this arena focus on developing technologies that ensure compliance with privacy regulations and ethical guidelines. This includes the creation of tagging systems that anonymize personal data, implement robust security measures, and provide transparency in how tags are generated and used.

Lastly, the role of R&D in advancing tagging practices is also evident in the field of healthcare. Accurate tagging of medical records, research data, and patient information can significantly improve the efficiency and quality of healthcare delivery. Through R&D, tagging systems can be developed to handle the complexity and sensitivity of medical data, ensuring that it is easily accessible to healthcare professionals while maintaining strict confidentiality and data integrity.

In conclusion, the role of Research and Development in advancing tagging practices is multifaceted and indispensable. From developing advanced algorithms and AI-driven systems to ensuring interoperability and enhancing user experience, R&D initiatives are at the forefront of making tagging practices more efficient, accurate, and user-friendly. Moreover, by addressing ethical and regulatory considerations, R&D ensures that the advancement of tagging practices is both responsible and sustainable.

# 21.4 Case Studies of Innovation in Tag Management

Innovation in tag management has become pivotal for businesses looking to enhance both their digital marketing strategies and analytical precision. This section delves into illustrative case studies that highlight how different organizations have effectively leveraged cutting-edge tag management solutions to streamline processes, improve data accuracy, and drive superior business outcomes.

One notable case study is from a multinational retail corporation that faced significant challenges with its outdated, fragmented tagging system. With an array of websites and an extensive range of products, the retailer struggled to maintain consistent and accurate data collection. This inconsistency led to erroneous data analytics, hampering their decision-making processes and marketing efforts. To address these issues, the company implemented an enterprise-level tag management system (TMS). By centralizing their tag management, they were able to ensure uniformity across all digital properties. Additionally, the ease of adding or modifying tags without requiring code changes on the website facilitated quicker marketing campaign launches and A/B testing. This innovation not only bolstered their analytical accuracy but also significantly reduced the time and resources traditionally spent on tag maintenance.

Another compelling example is found within a major financial services firm that wanted to optimize the user experience on its multiple online platforms. The firm's primary objective was to create a seamless, personalized customer journey while ensuring regulatory compliance, a particularly stringent requirement in the financial sector. By employing an advanced TMS equipped with built-in compliance checks, the company was able to manage and control data collection mechanisms more stringently. Moreover, the TMS enabled real-time tag deployment and deactivation, thereby enhancing flexibility while maintaining user privacy and data protection. This approach not only improved their operational efficiency but also instilled greater confidence among users about the security and reliability of the firm's online services.

In the context of media and entertainment, a leading global streaming service provider demonstrated the impact of innovative tag management in content recommendation and viewer engagement. With millions of viewers worldwide and an extensive library of content, the company faced the mammoth task of accurately tracking user preferences and viewing habits. The traditional tagging system was not robust enough to handle the complexities and exponential growth in user data. By transitioning to a dynamic TMS that used machine learning algorithms, the provider could dynamically tag content and automate the decision-making process for personalised recommendations. This sophisticated solution resulted in more accurate user profiling and enhanced viewer satisfaction. Moreover, the agility provided by the TMS allowed for rapid adjustments based on real-time data insights, ensuring that the recommendations remained relevant and engaging.

A significant innovation case in the automotive industry involves a leading car manufacturer that aimed to understand and influence the online purchasing behavior of its potential customers. The manufacturer used an analytical TMS to track intricate user interactions across its website, such as page views, clicks, and even the time spent on specific car models. By integrating these insights with their customer relationship management (CRM) system, they could create highly targeted marketing campaigns. This data-driven approach led to a marked improvement in lead generation and customer conversion rates. Furthermore, the TMS's ability to integrate seamlessly with various third-party marketing tools enabled the company to launch multichannel campaigns more efficiently, maximizing their outreach and impact.

Lastly, a large educational institution provides a groundbreaking instance of tag management innovation. The institution sought to enhance its online learning platforms' effectiveness and improve student engagement. They implemented a TMS that allowed for granular tracking of student activities such as course selection, content interaction, and progress. By analyzing this data, educators could identify learning patterns and bottlenecks, enabling them to tailor the educational content and user experience to better meet student needs. This led to improved course completion rates and higher student satisfaction levels. Additionally, the institution leveraged these insights to refine their recruitment strategies, attracting a more diverse and engaged student body.

In conclusion, these case studies underscore how innovative tag management can revolutionize various industries. From retail and finance to media, automotive, and education, organizations that adopt advanced TMS solutions are better positioned to enhance their data collection accuracy, optimize user experience, and ultimately drive more effective marketing and business strategies.

# 22. About the Author

Cybellium is dedicated to empowering individuals and organizations with the knowledge and skills they need to navigate the ever-evolving computer science landscape securely and learn only the latest information available on any subject in the category of computer science including:

- Information Technology (IT)

- Cyber Security

- Information Security

- Big Data

- Artificial Intelligence (AI)

- Engineering

- Robotics

- Standards and compliance

Our mission is to be at the forefront of computer science education, offering a wide and comprehensive range of resources, including books, courses, classes and training programs, tailored to meet the diverse needs of any subject in computer science.

Visit **https://www.cybellium.com** for more books

Made in the USA
Las Vegas, NV
07 December 2024

13556986R10138